Bloody, Bold and Resolute

Macbeth: Explained and Analysed

by Judy Darby

B.A. (Hons.) M.A. (Lond.S.O.A.S) M.A. (Lond. City University) B.Ed.

Published by New Generation Publishing in 2022

First Edition

ISBN

Paperback	978-1-80369-266-1
Ebook	978-1-80369-267-8

www.newgeneration-publishing.com

Macbeth

Contents

Introduction

It seems that I have always known the story of Macbeth for I first encountered it when I was about eight-years-old. My young self, reading *Tales from Shakespeare* by Charles and Mary Lamb, did not find ***Macbeth*** particularly grim for I had read the books my brothers read, and found the man with the hooded eyes in *The Thirty- Nine Steps,* and Blind Pew in *Treasure Island,* far more terrifying, the stuff of which nightmares were made. It was not until some years later that I realised that it was the blandness of the retold ***Macbeth*** story that had deceived me, for when I met the actual play when I was fourteen, at school, some of the horror began to hit me. Then, at A Level, ***Macbeth*** was on the set text list, and I began to study it in earnest, actually learning the play off by heart. I don't recommend that, because in the examination room I had too many quotations swirling round my head, although the learning by heart process strangely clarified anything I didn't totally understand.

This is a play that haunts me, and frequently I ask myself why this highly intelligent, imaginative character, knowing full well that the assassination of Duncan would bring him nothing but trouble and misery, nevertheless chose to go ahead? I have been teaching the play now for more years than I care to remember, and I ask students to ponder that question also. The answer lies in the ideas that Shakespeare might have borrowed from Aristotle although it is not certain that Shakespeare knew Aristotle's work. But Shakespeare certainly embraced some of the principles of tragedy set out by Aristotle, who defined tragedy as an *imitation of an action that is serious, complete, and of a certain magnitude.*[1]

---

[1] Aristotle *Poetics*

In classical Aristotelian Tragedy there are six principles that must be followed. We will look at three of these principles where ***Macbeth*** is concerned:

1. The tragic hero must be of royal or noble blood: *Macbeth was the king's cousin.*
2. The tragic hero must be of high standing in the community: *Macbeth was a renowned, fearless general, apparently totally loyal to the king.*
3. The tragic hero must have a fatal flaw*: Macbeth was overly ambitious.*

This fatal flaw would not only bring the tragic hero to destruction but would also hurt and destroy others who are innocent, in its wake. Macbeth's fatal flaw was the reason that he continued on a doomed enterprise. This flaw made him vulnerable to the machinations of the witches and the persuasion of his wife, but the responsibility for the assassination lies firmly with him: he committed the act.

The story of Macbeth is a dark one, and most of its themes are dominated by this darkness: tyranny, ruthlessness, savagery, cruelty, revenge and ignoble ambition. The sun shines only twice in this play, once when Duncan arrives at Inverness, at Macbeth's castle, [2]and again the impression of sunlight and summer is given when Malcolm arrives in Scotland with his army, and they cut down *leafy screens*.[3]

Macbeth is said to be the only Shakespeare play where the protagonists are happily married, but even so, we see the disintegration of this marriage when Macbeth's single minded ambition sets him on his own lonely, desperate course, and his wife is left without a rôle. She too has ambition, but it is not, as so many avow, for herself; her whole being is intent on securing the crown for her husband,

---

[2] Act 1 Scene 6

[3] Act 5 Scene 4

loyally supporting him even though she does not understand his tortured remorse and imagination.

I am writing this book in two parts: firstly I will be making the plot clear with supporting quotations explained. The intention is two-fold: those who find Shakespeare difficult to understand will be able to have a solid grasp of the plot and be able to support anything they write in examinations with the evidence supplied. It will also be valuable for those who are more confident as it is a straightforward thorough revision of the play. The second part of the book looks more closely at themes, characters and ideas, and analyses the significant soliloquies in detail. In no other Shakespeare play are we allowed such close access to the inner turmoil and meditations of the leading character in these rich, revealing soliloquies. Even Hamlet gives away fewer of his inner thoughts.

Plot isn't the main attraction of a Shakespeare play, and many of the plays do not have original story lines. Indeed, ***A Midsummer's Night's Dream*** is the only truly original Shakespeare play where plot is concerned. It is the language of Shakespeare that is magnificent, masterful and awe inspiring, converting the characters into figures whom we can often relate to, breathlessly wonder at, admire.

Such is the case with Macbeth. This man, part hero, part monster, is a man of such intense imagination that we can only admire and be aware of the appalling immensity of his actions, and wonder at his courage in going through with his terrible deeds. Lady Macbeth has little understanding of her husband's powerful and fearful imagination, and grows impatient with what she sees as unnecessary wavering and even cowardice. She is magnificent in her monstrosity, single minded, iron willed, but ultimately her inflexibility causes her to break, while the soldier, the man fearless in battle, fights to the final decisive moment, even when realising that he cannot win, that he has been seduced and tricked by those more devious than he.

Every time I read ***Macbeth***, I get something fresh from the pages, demonstrating the power and complexity of probably the greatest playwright the world has ever known. To all who study the play, I guarantee that they, too, will be rewarded by exciting, new insights each time they open the pages and immerse themselves in the beauty and wonder of Shakespeare's language. It is a gift that will remain throughout life, providing enjoyment, solace and satisfaction.

Part 1

The Story

In Act 1, Scene 1 we meet the witches amid thunder and lightning, highlighting how nature is disturbed by their presence. The histrionics would delight both Jacobean and modern audiences. The witches are deliberately ambiguous creatures; we are left to wonder whether they are male or female. When Banquo encounters them, he says:

You should be women, and yet your beards forbid me to interpret that you are so. [4]

The fact that Macbeth is mentioned by the witches cannot bode well for him, and at this stage the audience is left to conjecture whether this means he is a victim or whether he is in collusion with them, and is evil himself. We hear none of the characters refer to them as witches, but term them *weird women.* They refer to themselves as *weird women* also, although the first witch claims that the sailor's wife said, *Aroint thee witch,*[5] the only such reference.

We meet the witches on two further occasions: when they make their fateful prophecies to both Macbeth and Banquo, and again in Act 4 Scene 1, at Macbeth's instigation, although Hecate seems to have prior knowledge of his intention…*at the pit of Acheron…* (an entrance to hell) *thither he will come to know his destiny.* '[6]

The audience would accept the witches as credible, as this was an age when there was widespread belief in the supernatural as embodied in human beings, and James 1, recently crowned King of England, in addition to his title of James V1 of Scotland, the first of the Stuarts, had written a book on the subject, ***Daemonologie.***

---

[4] Act 1 Scene 3

[5] Act 1 Scene 3

[6] Act 3 Scene 5

The witches speak in rhyme which sets them apart from both serious and comic characters, although there is only one of the latter, the porter. Even his humour is muted and A.C. Bradley [7] believes that this is because Shakespeare viewed the tragedy as being too dark to allow anything more lighthearted.

The familiars of the witches were spirits who assisted them in their plots and spells. They usually took the form of animals, commonly cats, toads, frogs and birds. In this scene we only learn the names of two, Greymalkin, a cat, and Paddock, a toad. The third is named later, Harpier, just before the witches meet Macbeth at the pit of Acheron, and the name Harpier is a corruption of harpy from Greek mythology.

The witches are under the control of Hecate, goddess of the moon and witchcraft, and Hecate is angry when they involve themselves with Macbeth, as he has no interest in their art, only his own ambitions.

The witches have no power over Macbeth's actions, other than the power of suggestion and verbal deception, but that proves seductive as it aligns with his ambitions.

We witness the witches meeting only when the weather was unwelcoming, *thunder, lightning or in rain.* They thrive on chaos, contemplating *the hurly burly,* and *the battle,* speaking ambiguously and paradoxically. Their last rhyming couplet in this scene is an example of a type of paradox called chiasmus, where the phrase is turned on itself.

Act 1 Scene 2

Again, we hear of Macbeth without meeting him, and in this scene we learn of his courage and determination in battle.

Scotland was in a parlous state, with Duncan being threatened by three enemies.

---

[7] A.C. Bradley Shakespearean Tragedy

We hear of Macdonwald first: totally *merciless* with *multiplying villainies of nature*, clearly a powerful force. He had obtained mercenaries to fight for him: *kerns and gallowglasses*. Kerns were lightly armed foot soldiers, probably impoverished Irish men, while gallowglasses were horsemen armed with axes, a terrifying prospect.

At first the situation was doubtful but then Macbeth made his move. With the personification that Shakespeare uses so freely, Macbeth's courage is extolled, as the sergeant views him as *Valour's minion* as he *carv'd out his passage,* a gruesome image, before he *unseamed him from the nave to the chaps*, and then put Macdonwald's head on the battlements.

With Banquo, Macbeth then takes on the King of Norway and his ally, the treacherous Thane of Cawdor, but again it is Macbeth who reaps the praise, likened to *Bellona's bridegroom*, an allusion to Mars, the Roman god of war.

This scene displays the violent nature of Macbeth, his ruthlessness and determination, all acceptable qualities in the Scotland of the time when used in the service of the king. Duncan refers to him as *valiant cousin, worthy gentleman,* and *noble Macbeth.* The problem, of course, will be when Macbeth turns his viciousness against the king himself in order to fulfil his craving for the highest position in the land. He himself will term this craving as *vaulting ambition*[8], fully aware of the inevitable result.

Act 1 Scene 3

Once again we meet the witches, and the air is disturbed by thunder. We witness their vindictiveness when the first witch vows to take revenge on a sailor's wife, who refused to give her the chestnuts she was eating. The witch declares that she will sail to Aleppo *in a sieve,* and torment the sailor, who is *master o'the Tiger,* with winds controlled by all three

[8] Act 1 Scene 7

witches. His torture will last *seven nights nine times nine* and he will have no rest throughout that time as his ship will be *tempest tossed.* She cannot scupper his ship as traditionally witches did not have that power.

The witches are apparently close in friendship. The first witch tells the second, *Th'rt kind,* and they walk round *hand in hand* just before Macbeth and Banquo enter.

Macbeth's opening words are startling in that they are evocative of the witches' words in the first scene of the play. However, his comment *so foul and fair a day I have not seen* has very different connotations from the witches' pronouncement, as he is alluding to the weather and to the day's success.

The witches make it clear that they wish to speak to Macbeth, and it is at this stage he hears the words which will prove fatal to his peace of mind from then right up to his death. The witches pronounce him Thane of Glamis, Thane of Cawdor and *king hereafter.*

Banquo's query as to why Macbeth seems so startled and fearful of *things that do sound so fair* causes us to wonder also, and there seems to be credible evidence later in this scene and when Lady Macbeth taunts him, that Macbeth had already thought about regicide, and is rather more than uneasy when the possibility is mentioned by the witches, as his dreams are offered reality.

Banquo is keen to discover what the witches prophesy for him while claiming not to *beg nor fear your favours nor your hate*. Later, we are to discover that Banquo takes to heart what the witches forecast for him, and how his reaction has a bearing on his death.

The witches tell him: *Thou shalt get kings though thou be none*, and we also discover later, that this prediction for Banquo concerns Macbeth greatly.

A dramatic turn is taken with Ross and Angus arriving to tell Macbeth that Duncan wishes to honour him with the title of Thane of Cawdor, as the previous one has been condemned to death for treason. Macbeth's puzzled reaction puzzles us also until we realise that Macbeth did not come face to face with Cawdor in the battles, only with Macdonwald and the King of Norway. In the chaos and tumult it is possible that he did not know of Cawdor's role, for as Ross states, it was unknown whether his forces were combined with Norway's, or whether he merely supplied Norway with troops and advantages, but *treasons capital, confessed and proved, have overthrown him.*

Macbeth's immediate reaction is to tell himself that *the greatest is behind* and we wonder at a man who can think the acquisition of two Thane titles, one of which was hereditary, has any comparison with what he would have to do to become king. He is probably already troubled by the prediction given to Banquo that his children *shall be kings* but preoccupied by his own vivid, terrible imagination, something that will plague and haunt him for the rest of his aborted life. His own thoughts make his hair stand on end and his heart *knock at my ribs against the use of nature.*

Act 1 Scene 4

At the beginning of this scene we discover that the Thane of Cawdor has been executed and that he died in great remorse, begging the king's forgiveness. Malcolm tells Duncan, *Nothing in his life became him like the leaving it.*

Duncan's reaction is ironic for the audience, as we are already aware of Macbeth's ambition. The king declares:

There's no art
To find the mind's construction in the face.
He was a gentleman on whom I built
An absolute trust.

The first Cawdor we hear of in this play rebels against him; the second one will murder him.

When Macbeth and Banquo arrive, Duncan expresses his gratitude in hyperbolic terms, but this is a portrayal of a genuine, honourable king. No character in this play utters one word of criticism about him. This does not concur with the historical account of Duncan, but clearly Shakespeare was more than aware of James 1's ancestry and how unwise it would be to offend the king.

Duncan chooses this amount to announce that his heir will be his eldest son, Malcolm, something that Macbeth laments in an aside:

The Prince of Cumberland. That is a step
On which I must fall down, or else o'erleap,
For in my way it lies.

His ambition is not weakened as he pleads, *Let not light see my black and deep desires.*

Ironically, as Macbeth leaves the king, with murderous thoughts in his mind, to go ahead to Inverness to tell his wife that the king will stay with them that night, Duncan is singing his praises to Banquo: *he is full so valiant...a peerless kinsman.*

Act 1 Scene 5

In this scene we meet Lady Macbeth for the first time. She is reading a letter sent by her husband telling of his encounter with the witches. Lady Macbeth is delighted and determined, declaring, *Glamis thou art and Cawdor, and shalt be what thou art promised.* Throughout the play her ambition is for her husband alone; we never hear her show ambition for herself. We learn about Macbeth's character from her viewpoint when she comments in detail on what she perceives as weaknesses. He is *too full o' th' milk of human kindness* to do what was necessary to become king, and does not want *the illness* (wickedness) that also goes with such a deed. She acknowledges that her husband is ambitious, but what he values highly he wishes to achieve in a moral manner, yet also thinks that he would accept the rewards of a murder done by someone else. She is anxious that Macbeth should hasten home so that she can convince him, and verbally reject *all that impedes thee from the golden round.*

Lady Macbeth is ecstatic when she learns that Duncan is coming to their castle, and immediately associates that with his demise*: the raven itself is hoarse that croaks the fatal entrance of Duncan under my battlements.* Ravens are birds of ill-omen, and Lady Macbeth follows this with calling on evil spirits to *unsex me here* in order to make her strong and lethal. She asks to be filled from *crown* to *the toe* with *direst cruelty*, and *take my milk for gall,* a bitter substance. Just as Macbeth had not wished the stars to witness his black, murderous action, she is anxious that her *keen knife* should not witness the *wound it makes.* Perhaps even at this early stage she is showing signs of the weakness, for which she has great contempt when she sees it in her husband.

On Macbeth's arrival she greets him by both his titles, and her excitement is almost tangible: *greater than both by all the all-hail hereafter* (allusion to becoming king) and she adds, *Thy letters have transported me beyond the ignorant present.* It is interesting to note that *letters* is in the plural. Had he written more on the subject of his ambitions to her?

Lady Macbeth's ominous comment, *O never shall sun that morrow see,* when she learns that Duncan intends departing the next day, tells us that she intends the king to be murdered that night, and she quickly follows that comment with admonishment to Macbeth that he must not look so transparent. She likens his face to a book *where man may read strange matters.* He has to learn the art of deception by acting normally and be *like th'innocent flower but be the serpent under't.* She is eager to organise the murder herself, calling it *the night's great business* as if she does not trust him to carry the murder out unaided and directed by her.

Interestingly, do we note a touch of hesitation in Macbeth with his comment, *We will speak further*? Does he sound almost reluctant? The urgent, fearful ambition of earlier scenes seems to have faded. If so, his wife is oblivious as she states firmly, *Leave all the rest to me.*

Act 1 Scene 6

Duncan arrives at Macbeth's castle at Inverness and he and Banquo are full of praise for its setting as it *nimbly and sweetly* affects the senses. It would seem to the audience that Duncan is coming to Paradise to be slaughtered.

Lady Macbeth offers fulsome, hypocritical compliments to the king when she welcomes him, and he asks to be taken to Macbeth whom, he declares, *we love…highly.*

This brief scene illustrates the innocence and benevolence of Duncan and the callous, cynical attitude of Lady Macbeth.

Act 1 Scene 7

This is a vital scene in which Macbeth leaves the feast to be on his own and soliloquise about murdering Duncan. In his soliloquy[9] we witness Macbeth's doubts about murdering the king for the first time, although in an earlier scene, (Act 1 Scene 5) his ambiguous words to Lady Macbeth, *we will speak further,* could well reflect his indecision. He comes to the conclusion that Duncan is a great king, and that all he has in his favour is *vaulting ambition.*

However, it will only take a few minutes of well-chosen insults from his wife to change Macbeth's mind, and as he is a tragic hero, fulfilling the criteria for that role, [10] it is inevitable that he will murder Duncan.

Lady Macbeth comes to find him and has a powerful reaction to the news that her husband wishes to *proceed no further in this business,* accusing him of cowardice, and of being drunk when he first proposed the murder of Duncan. This accusation is interesting as we have not seen Macbeth suggest the murder to his wife: thus we can infer that such a conversation took place in the past. Lady Macbeth also

---

[9] Analysis of soliloquy page 34
[10] See page 1

uses emotional blackmail, telling her husband that from that moment *such I account thy love*, and she taunts him with the fact that he would always know that he was a coward, afraid to murder, although wanting the crown, like a cat who wanted fish but was afraid to dip his paws into a pond and get them wet. She knows her husband well, and his reaction to accusations of cowardice is one of anger:

Prithee, peace!
I dare do all that may become a man,
Who dares do more is none.

Lady Macbeth has not finished. She continues to insult his masculinity, something very hard for this man of action to take, and also refers again to what might well have been an earlier conversation on the subject, when she says that previously he was willing to find place and opportunity even though neither was available. Lady Macbeth shocks with her next utterly ruthless comment, declaring that if she had broken a vow as he intends to do, she would have taken a baby while feeding it at her breast and *dashed the brains out.* Macbeth begins to submit to her wishes, and then she also explains how she will drug Duncan's guards, and the *spongy officers* can be blamed for the murder.

Macbeth does not react with shock, but instead admiration, for the Jacobean masculine qualities she is displaying, urging his wife to *bring forth male children only.* Her powerful persuasion has overcome all his doubts and scruples and he is now determined to see the evil deed through to its conclusion, again declaring the intention to put on a *false face* to hide his *false heart.*

Act 2 Scene 1

In this scene we discover that Banquo has been more disturbed by the witches' prophecies with regard to him than was previously apparent. He comments on the thriftiness of heaven: *their candles are all out* before revealing that he is unwilling to sleep despite being exhausted because of the thoughts that torture him:

Merciful powers, restrain in me the cursed thoughts that nature
Gives way to in repose.

However, when Macbeth joins him he makes conversation about Duncan having been *in unusual pleasure* about the evening's celebration, and we are once more reminded of Duncan's generosity when we learn that he has sent money to Macbeth's servants and wishes Lady Macbeth, his *most kind hostess* to have a diamond to show his gratitude.

Banquo seems anxious to talk about the witches to Macbeth, and in contrast to his dismissal of their words when he and Macbeth encountered them on the heath, he now admits he dreamed about them the previous night and comments that they *have showed some truth* to Macbeth.

Macbeth's immediate reaction is to deny thinking about the witches but adds that when they have the time they could discuss the matter. He adds that when they do it would be profitable for Banquo if he takes Macbeth's advice.

It would seem that Banquo has reservations and possible suspicions when he hears that, and he states quite firmly that he will do so as long as he *can keep my bosom franchised, and allegiance clear* meaning his conscience and duty to the king must not be compromised. It is clear that Banquo is honourable and loyal to Duncan and has no hesitation in making Macbeth well aware of where his loyalties lie.

With the departure of Banquo and Fleance, Macbeth is left alone to ponder uneasily on what the night will bring. We know from his instruction to the servant that Lady Macbeth will be ringing a bell when the coast is clear for him to murder the king.

Hallucination and a cruel imagination play a major role in Macbeth's doubts and inner turmoil, and in the soliloquy which follows both are strongly evident.[11]

Macbeth's frustration at being unable to grasp the dagger is vividly portrayed through the sense of sight, and he even draws his own dagger to emphasise this. However, his frustration subsides when he realises that it is *the bloody business* which causes the hallucination and moves on to ponder on night being the appropriate background to murder. He muses on witchcraft and the goddess of the moon and witchcraft, Hecate, and likens himself to Sexton Tarquinius, the son of a Roman ruler who raped the wife of a noble Roman, causing her to commit suicide.

The change in Macbeth from the noble, acclaimed man at the beginning of the play, is marked. We now see him comparing himself to someone wicked without remorse, and embracing the silence which *suits* the *present horror of the time.* Abruptly, he stops his reflections to concentrate on what lies ahead: *Whiles I threat, he lives*, and concludes that too much talking reduces his desire to act. As often with a significant scene, Shakespeare finishes with a rhyming couplet when he hears Lady Macbeth ringing the bell:

Hear it not, Duncan, for it is a knell,
That summons thee to heaven, or to hell.

Later in the play, after planning Banquo's murder, Macbeth comments in similar vein:

Banquo, thy soul's flight,
If it find heaven, must find it out tonight. [12]

---

[11] Analysis of soliloquy page 36
[12] Act 3 Scene 1

Act 2 Scene 2

As she concludes her preparations for the murder we see an anxious, jittery Lady Macbeth, another sign of the weakness that she tries to suppress. She says that she could have murdered Duncan herself if it wasn't for the fact that he looked so like her father as he slept. She hears an owl shriek and that startles her also and calls the bird *the fatal bellman*, an allusion to the bell rung outside the cell of a condemned man the night before execution.

Even at this stage in the play the signs are there that Lady Macbeth is not as strong as she presents. Firstly, she had asked for the aid of evil spirits: thus it can be inferred that she did not feel she could go through with such a terrible deed unaided, and now her nerves are frayed to such an extent that when Macbeth calls out to her she thinks they have been caught in the act, not realising at that moment that it is her husband.

Husband and wife then indulge in the quick exchange of words termed stichomythia, displaying their agitation, but Lady Macbeth pulls herself together quickly, having little patience with Macbeth's stark fear of what he has done and how it has alienated him from God (hardly surprising when he had murdered God's deputy).

When Macbeth pours out his lyrical words on sleep, culminating in:

Balm of hurt minds, great nature's second course,
Chief nourisher in life's feast,

his wife can only respond with *What do you mean?* clearly demonstrating the great gulf between their imagination and understanding.

Helplessly, and in anguish he cries out:

Glamis hath murdered sleep, and therefore Cawdor
Shall sleep no more. Macbeth shall sleep no more.

The use of all three titles is all encompassing, for him there is no escape and no more rest.

Macbeth is filled with remorse; her response is brutal ~ *infirm of purpose* ~ and she tells him he is thinking *brainsickly.* Lady Macbeth sees things very simply, that water will clean the blood from their hands, so *how easy is it then.* She has no comprehension of his mental torture and conscience, and Shakespeare paints her as inflexible, lacking imagination and morality. But her inflexibility will prove to be her undoing, because what cannot bend must break when the pressure is too great. She devotes her life to supporting her husband, her ambitions are all for him, and when this begins to unravel, when she is no longer his confidante, her purpose in life disappears.

By the end of the scene we are left in wonder at a man who sees very clearly the enormity of his actions, who knew that enormity before he murdered the king, and who knows that he will suffer for that for what remains of his life.

Act 2 Scene 3

Shakespeare's tragedies all contain comic scenes, and ***Macbeth*** has just one, the grimly dark Porter's scene. The knocking that troubled Macbeth at the end of the last scene ~ *wake Duncan with thy knocking. I would thou couldst* ~ is the knocking that has disturbed the Porter and is the prelude to Duncan's body being found by Macduff, who enters as an avenging angel.

In medieval times, hell would be represented as a castle with a porter to let sinners in, and this representation is used by Shakespeare in this scene. The Porter imagines that he is a hell-porter and describes three likely candidates for admission before he tires of the game, declaring, *this place is too cold for hell.*

The first person he pretends to admit is a farmer, who, anticipating a good harvest, hanged himself as he would not be able to charge so much and therefore have less profit. The second is an equivocator, someone who could speak ambiguously to deliberately mislead, and it is thought that Shakespeare is referring to the case of the Jesuit Garnet who went on trial for his part in the Gunpowder Plot of 1605. Equivocation is alluded to several times in this play, and perhaps the most dramatic moment is when Macbeth realises that the witches have deceived him with their ambiguity: *That palter with us in a double sense.* [13] Equivocation is raised in the conversation between Lady Macduff and her son, although he points out to his mother that there are more people who *swear and lie*[14] than honest men.

The third is a reference to the practice of some English tailors to remake French leggings into the closer fitting English style, thus stealing the extra material. *Here you may roast your goose*, the Porter puns, alluding to the shape of the tailor's iron with its long goose neck shape.

As he stops imagining people he could have admitted to hell, the Porter cynically comments, *I had thought to let in some of all professions that go the primrose way to the everlasting bonfire.*

The persistent knocking finally causes the Porter to open the door, but not before he has asked the unknown caller to remember to tip him. Macduff and Lennox are waiting and Macduff greets him cordially while asking if he had gone to bed late as the Porter has had to be roused.

Then follows some funny, crude comments from the Porter about the effects of alcohol which *provoke(s) nose-painting, sleep and urine* with its persuasive and disheartening qualities. Another reference to equivocation is made when the Porter comments on its influence on sexual performance, in that alcohol provides the desire but takes away the ability, and then *equivocates him in a sleep.*

The Porter sees his encounter with drink as a battle, one which he wins with his comment on being sick: after he had fallen over in his drunkenness he *made shift to cast him.*

---

[13] Act 5 Scene 7

[14] Act 4 Scene 2

The comedy is not to last. Macduff greets Macbeth courteously with *worthy thane* and recognises the fact that being host to the king is *a joyful trouble...but yet 'tis one.* As Macduff goes to wake Duncan Lennox relates how *unruly* the night had been, and the vivid, powerful description of Nature in turmoil together with:

Strange screams of death,
And prophesying, with accents terrible

predicts that there will be confusion and chaos.

Lennox has never experienced anything like it. Macbeth's response is muted, and we can only imagine how Lennox' s words play on his already tortured remorse.

Macduff's reappearance, and his stark horror at what he has discovered is expected but nonetheless shocking. His words are evocative of the fact that the king is God's deputy, that this is *most sacrilegious murder* and that Duncan's body is *the Lord's anointed temple*. He also uses the mythical Gorgon to emphasise the enormity of the murder, a monster who turned anyone who looked at her to stone. More religious allusion is made when Macduff likens the murder to *the great doom's image*, the Last Judgement, when the dead rise to be judged by their maker.

Lady Macbeth's sense of what is appropriate in certain situations deserts her when she reacts to Macduff's revelation. Her *what in our house*? receives a stern rebuke from Banquo. His friendship with Macduff is obvious *(Dear Duff)* and his plea, *pr'ythee contradict thyself* demonstrates his shock and grief. Does he immediately consider that Macbeth is responsible? It would be hard to think otherwise after their meeting with the witches, and the fact that Duncan is under Macbeth's roof and therefore more easily accessible.

Macbeth's first speech after the discovery comes from his heart. We already are aware of his state of mind and his guilt and remorse, and now he blurts out that if he had died an hour before this event then he would have lived *a blessed time.* For him, from now on, nothing matters, everything is trivial, and all that is left of *the wine of life* is *the mere lees* or dregs, a bitter sediment.

However, when the suspicious Macduff asks him why he had killed the guards, his speech is hyperbolic and sophistic, asking who would be able to be *wise, amazed, temperate, and furious, loyal and neutral, in a moment?* He describes Duncan's body as being breached *for ruin's wasteful entrance,* and finishes with another rhetorical question:

Who could refrain,
That had a heart to love, and in that heart
Courage to make love known?

Whether Lady Macbeth really faints at that juncture is unknown as Shakespeare makes no indication, but it is debatable. Either this is another sign that she is not as strong as she appears, or she wishes to create a diversion to take the attention away from Macbeth, which could imply that she is aware that there are those who suspect him. Her protective instincts where her husband is concerned are very strong.

There is general agreement that everyone should dress, *our naked frailties hid* before meeting to discuss what Banquo describes as *this most bloody piece of work* and he vows to fight the *treasonous malice.*

Left alone, Malcolm and Donalbain agree that their safety is at stake and decide to leave for England and Ireland respectively, and to do so immediately without being *dainty of leave-taking.*

Act 2 Scene 4

This is a scene which Shakespeare used to keep the audience informed of what is going on away from the main protagonists. The conversation between Ross and an old man reveals that nature is very disturbed for there is an eclipse of the sun as *dark night strangles the travelling lamp.* Ross wonders whether day is too ashamed to show its face after Duncan's murder, and both men ponder on the terrible events that have happened since, such as the king's horses eating each other and a falcon being hawked at by a mousing owl. All is unnatural just as the assassination had been.

Macduff's appearance tells us that Macbeth has been named as the next king and has gone to Scone to be *invested* as such. Duncan's body has been taken to Colmekill for burial. We also learn that Macduff will not be going to the coronation, confirming that he suspects Macbeth of Duncan's murder.

Act 3 Scene 1

Banquo's soliloquy reveals why he has said nothing so far, and puts him in a less honourable light. Although his firm comment to Macbeth on the night of the king's murder made it clear that he would not do anything to harm Duncan, here we become aware that his own ambitions are powerful. Thus, although he *fears* that Macbeth *play'dst most foully* he is quick to consider the benefits in that he is predicted to *be the root and father many kings.*

Banquo's musings are interrupted by the arrival of Macbeth, who is now king, and Lady Macbeth with their entourage, including the ubiquitous Ross. When Macbeth learns that Banquo is going riding he is very interested to learn how far and when he will be back, and that Banquo's son Fleance will be with him.

Fail not our feast, Macbeth orders.

My lord, I will not. Banquo's words are to prove ironic.

We are offered more information about Malcolm and Donalbain's whereabouts, for they have reached England and Ireland with their accounts which Macbeth dismisses as *strange invention.*

The meeting with the murderers that follows, indicates how totally ruthless, manipulative and calculating Macbeth has become. He is hell-bent on ridding himself of Banquo, and in his soliloquy[15] which prefaces the meeting we learn how fearful, bitter and desperate his thoughts are. It is a surprise to hear that he fears Banquo's *royalty of nature* as that has not been evident so far in the play, but no surprise to learn that the witches' predictions for Banquo torment him.

Macbeth's manipulation of the murderers is masterful. The assertion, *We are men, my liege* makes it clear how Macbeth has roused their desire for revenge, ironically against the wrong man. His extended metaphor, where he compares the qualities of different breeds of dogs with those of men is seductive, especially with the added bonus of earning the favour of the king and the subsequent rewards.

Secrecy and immediacy are urged upon the murderers, and the need also to murder Fleance, Banquo's son. It becomes evident that Banquo's hours are numbered.

Act 3 Scene 2

Lady Macbeth is no longer happy. Why she has changed her attitude is not altogether clear except it is very apparent that what the two of them have achieved has brought her no satisfaction.

She comments that nothing has been gained, everything wasted, and that *'tis safer to be that which we destroy, than by destruction dwell in doubtful joy.* This comes as a shock to the audience for she has changed from single-minded ruthlessness to regret about their actions, even feeling that she would be better dead.

What is particularly interesting about this is that as soon as Macbeth joins her she urges him to forget what they have done, for if nothing can be done about a situation then it should be forgotten. *What's done is done*, she insists, in marked reversal from what she has said when alone.

---

[15] Soliloquy analysed on page 37

Macbeth, who does not seem to feel his wife needs protecting in the same way that she protects him, pours out his feelings, and they are virtually identical to the ones we have just observed her reveal:

Better be with the dead,
Whom we, to gain our peace, have sent to peace.

Once again, we see a wife, ambitious for her husband, but also fiercely protective of his mental state, hide her own feelings in order to cheer him. He hints that that he has plans for Banquo, but Lady Macbeth has changed and now shows only a passing interest.

Act 3 Scene 3

This brief scene is where Banquo is murdered as he nears the castle. To make certain of success Macbeth has sent a third murderer to join the pair, but even so they fail to kill Fleance, and he makes his escape.

Act 3 Scene 4

This banquet scene makes clear how fragile Macbeth's emotional state has become. We can almost feel sorry for Lady Macbeth as she strives to prevent Macbeth from revealing the truth. Once he has discovered that Fleance is still alive he becomes agitated: *I am cabined, cribbed, confined, bound in to saucy doubts and fears,* but it is the knowledge of Banquo's death, although planned, that causes him to hallucinate and see the ghost.

Lady Macbeth desperately tries to convince the thanes that his outpourings are due to a recurring illness and are nothing to worry about, while at the same time she tries to calm Macbeth and jolt him back to sanity. She rebukes him sharply:

This is the very painting of your fear.
This is the air-drawn dagger which you said
Led you to Duncan.

Mindful of the fact that the murderer had told him that Banquo had received *twenty trenched gashes on his head*, Macbeth muses that in the past men would die when their *brains were out*:

But now they rise again,
With twenty mortal murders on their crowns.

There is a touch of black comedy in his complaint, *and push us from our stools.* He is confused and unnerved, and asserts that if Banquo was in the form of a *rugged Russian bear* or *Hyrcan tiger* or even alive again, challenging him to a sword fight, he would not be afraid or 'tremble'. But he cannot cope with the *horrible shadow*, the name for a ghost.

As Macbeth's state of mind deteriorates yet further Lady Macbeth realises that the situation is dangerous, for Macbeth has said too much already. When a bemused Ross asks, *What sights my lord?* Lady Macbeth acts swiftly:

Stand not upon the order of your going,
But go at once.

She has striven to keep Macbeth from uttering damning comments and to restore him to normality, but has failed. When we consider that she herself is feeling depressed about what they have done, her efforts are heroic. She has the capacity to do what he cannot, to be unswerving and consistent, and not allow fanciful and fearful imagination control her words and actions in public. Yet, this same iron and rigid self control will finally break.

After their guests have gone she no longer chastises him, but simply sounds very weary, telling him that he *lacks the season of all natures sleep.* Perhaps she is remembering

Macbeth's words after the murder: *Macbeth shall sleep no more.*

Macbeth is preoccupied by the fact that Macduff has ignored his command to come to court, and reveals the fact that he has spies in all the nobles' houses. He is increasingly suspicious and wary. He decides to visit the witches to discover *by the worst means* (witchcraft) what lies in store for him. He realises that there is no going back as he has committed such terrible murders and is so steeped in blood that *'should I wade no more,*

Returning were as tedious as go o'er'.

After the horrific hallucination of Banquo he is now calm and resolved, deciding that he is a beginner in murder and needs practice or *hard use.*

Act 3 Scene 5

This is a scene that was probably added at a later date by Thomas Middleton, when it was revised by him for Shakespeare's company, the King's Men.

In this scene Hecate is angry with the witches for not only engaging with a *wayward son* who *loves for his own ends and not for you,* but also for not involving her *the mistress of (their) charms.*

However, all is not lost as Macbeth will be meting them the next day at the pit of Acheron and the witches are instructed to meet there complete with their vessels, charms and spells. Hecate herself will spend the night planning evil and lethal schemes. She will also provide artificial spirits and illusions to lure him to destruction. Macbeth would become so convinced that:

He shall spurn fate, scorn death, and bear
His hopes 'bove wisdom, grace and fear.

These are ominous words and Hecate concludes that such security *is mortals' chiefest enemy.*

Act 3 Scene 6

Another scene in which Shakespeare uses minor characters to give us further insight into the situation.

Lennox and a lord are discussing what has happened since Duncan's death. We learn that Macbeth has accused Malcolm, Donalbain and Fleance of the murders of their fathers. The tone is ironic and it takes a little while for us to realise that the two men do not believe Macbeth's lies:

That had he Duncan's sons under his key,
(As an't please heaven, he shall not) they should find
What 'twere to kill a father. So should Fleance.

They discuss Macduff and how he is *in disgrace* because he had refused to attend *the tyrant's feast,* and also that he has gone to England to ask for King Edward's assistance to overthrow Macbeth so that:

we may again
Give to our tables meat, sleep to our nights,
Free from our feasts and banquets bloody knives.

The two men also comment that Macduff would need to be wary and hope that blessing returns to *suffering* Scotland which is *under a hand accursed.*

Act 4 Scene 1

This is a crucial scene in the play. Macbeth seeks to learn what fate has in store for him.

Firstly, the witches assemble and prepare their evil potions and spells, chanting in rhyme throughout:

For a charm of powerful trouble,
Like a hell-broth, boil and bubble.

Ironically, the witches chant that *something wicked* is coming. By whose standards? Macbeth's greeting is far from polite when he says, *How now you secret, black and midnight hags,* and his impassioned speech which follows illustrates his desperation, as he declares that the world can be thrown into chaos *even till destruction sicken* as long as he gets the answers he seeks.

The witches are amenable to his request. It is clear that Banquo's wise words about evil spirits winning their prey over with *honest trifles* [16] are now coming to pass. The warning and predictions which follow are listened to carefully, Macbeth believing every word.

He is warned, *Beware Macduff! Beware the Thane of Fife*! This is a clever warning as Macbeth is already fearful and suspicious of Macduff, who neither attended his coronation nor his feast, ignoring the summons.

However, he is the assured that *none of woman born shall harm Macbeth.* This delights him, but so far has Macbeth progressed down his destructive path, that he has no hesitation in deciding that nevertheless he will have Macduff put to death to *make assurance double sure.*

The second prediction the witches make is that Macbeth cannot be beaten

> *Until*
> *Great Birnam wood to high Dunsinane hill*
> *Shall come against him.*

Macbeth is still not satisfied even though he calls the predictions *sweet bodements, good,* and is convinced that now he will live his natural life-span. But he is also desperate to know if Banquo's heirs will ever rule Scotland. He threatens an *eternal curse* on them if they do not tell him. There is a certain irony in Macbeth talking of cursing those who curse, just as there was in the witches terming him *wicked.*

---

[16] Act 1 Scene 3

What Macbeth is shown fills him with horror. A procession of eight kings, the last one holding a mirror, is followed by the ghost of Banquo, *blood bolstered.* and he cannot cope with what he sees. *I'll see no more…horrible sight!*

More curses, this time the *pernicious hour*, and Macbeth emerges to discover that Macduff has fled to England. Out of his fury comes a vicious resolve: as he cannot kill Macduff, he will slaughter his wife and children instead. The hero of recent times has become a monster.

Act 4 Scene 2

This is a poignant scene where we see a justifiably anxious Lady Macduff questioning why her husband has fled from Scotland. She resents the fact that he has left her and sees it as reckless desertion. Despite all the efforts of Ross to defend Macduff, saying, *He is noble, wise, judicious, and best knows the fits o' the season,* referring to the terrible violence of Macbeth at this time, Lady Macduff is not reassured. She considers Macduff's action as a betrayal of his family, leaving wife and children unprotected, for even the wren, *the most diminutive of birds* will fight to protect her young from the predatory owl.

Ross does not stay around to help Lady Macduff after he has commented on the cruelty of times in which men *are traitors and do not know ourselves.* He tells her that he will come again, and moved by Lady Macbeth's words about her son, in that *fathered he is and yet he's fatherless,* he leaves.

There follows banter between Lady Macduff and her delightfully precocious son, and our sympathy is with this family as we wait for the inevitable slaughter, which we have been warned to expect in the previous scene when Macbeth vows to destroy Macduff's family.

The warning from the messenger, although well meant, is futile as it would be impossible for Lady Macduff to escape with her children. We have to assume that there are no strong body guards in this castle, that security is sorely lacking. She dies bravely and defiantly when she says in response to their demands for her husband's whereabouts:

I hope in no place so unsanctified
Where such as thou may find him.

Her son also displays courage when he denies that his father is a traitor, saying, *Thou liest, thou shag-eared villain.*

He tries to protect his mother by telling her to run even as he realises that he is dying, and once again it is brought home forcibly just how vicious and evil Macbeth has become.

Act 4 Scene 3

Macduff has arrived in England and is talking to a wary Malcolm. Macduff urges him *like good men* to *bestride our downfall'n birthdom.* He reminds him of all the horror and sorrow which is being endured by Scotland and personifies Heaven in its sympathy with the country.

Malcolm is blunt in response, commenting that Macduff has loved Macbeth *well* and that he hasn't been touched by Macbeth yet. In fact, it is possible that Macduff might be willing to offer him up to the king. Malcolm visualises himself as *a weak, poor innocent lamb* being sacrificed to propitiate *an angry god.*

Despite Macduff's protests that he is not treacherous Malcolm is not convinced as even a good man might give way to a king's command. However, he concedes that just because some are evil that doesn't mean that all are: *Angels are bright still, though the brightest fell* and although evil people put on a good façade, those who are genuinely good also seem good.

Macduff feels rebuffed and Malcolm continues relentlessly by asking why he left his wife and children unprotected, *those strong knots of love.* Nevertheless, yet again he concedes that Macduff *may be rightly just.* Whatever Macduff might have been expecting when he went to England it unlikely that he thought he would be met with suspicion. He reacts emotionally and in despair:

Bleed, bleed poor country!
Great tyranny, lay thy basis sure...
... Fare thee well, lord.

His pride is hurt at being thought such a villain, and his despair is triggered at the thought of Scotland having no justified royal opposition to Macbeth.

Malcolm, termed *a more Machiavellian version of Duncan*[17] now tests Macduff by claiming to have more vices than Macbeth, even though Macbeth is *smacking of every sin that has a name.* Among these sins is the accusation *luxurious* which surprises us as the Jacobean meaning is lustful, something we haven't witnessed, rather a man devoted to his wife.

The sins Malcolm claims to have are those of *voluptuousness* which Macduff, although disapproving, thinks can be managed with *willing dames* which is a sad commentary on the Jacobean attitude towards women. Then Malcolm says that he also has a *staunchless avarice* but once more, Macduff, desperate for Malcolm to return to Scotland and overthrow Macbeth, is willing to accept it as Scotland has enough wealth to cope, and the situation can be managed if Malcolm has other *graces.* But Malcolm denies this, declaring that he has no *king- becoming graces:* on the contrary he enjoys varieties of crimes and he will destroy all peace and *confound all unity on earth.*

Macduff's reaction is powerful: *Fit to govern? No, not to live.*

He is in despair asking when Scotland would see *wholesome days again,* inveighing against Malcolm dishonouring his family, his father *a sainted king* and his mother, the queen, *oft'ner upon her knees than on her feet.*

For Macduff all hope for Scotland and himself has gone.

---

[17] Carolyn Asp

Malcolm is now totally convinced that Macduff is genuine. He explains to the *child of integrity* that Macbeth has been sending people to lure him back under the pretence of friendship. But he now wishes to put himself into Macduff's hands and take back the accusations he has made against himself.

Malcolm then explains that he is a virgin *unknown to women,* that he has never broken a vow or promise, hardly desires his own possessions and delights in truthfulness. His first lie was the one against himself, and he was ready to serve Macduff and his country. Before Macduff arrived, Siward and ten thousand men were ready to go to Scotland, to battle.

A bemused Macduff says:

Such welcome and unwelcome things at once
'Tis hard to reconcile.

At this stage in the scene Shakespeare introduces the information about *the evil,* and the gift Edward has to cure a terrible skin condition. With prayers the king puts a gold coin around the neck of the afflicted person. It is *a most miraculous work* and the gift is passed to his descendants. This is one of the scenes in the play where Shakespeare is deliberately pleasing James 1, who could trace his line back to Edward, although it would be difficult to imagine James, who was not renowned for altruism, attempting the cure.

Now there is a grim turn in events after the hope inspired by Edward's support, and Siward's leadership of an English force. Ross arrives with the tragic news that Macduff's wife and children have been slaughtered. Malcolm urges him to *make med'cines of our great revenge* and to *dispute it like a man.* Macduff's response is from the heart: *I must also feel it like a man.* His remorse is overwhelming as he cries, *Sinful Macduff, they were all struck for thee!*

Macduff 's resolve to gain revenge is powerful:

Front to front bring thou this fiend of Scotland and myself.

Malcolm is approving*: This tune goes manly.*

Early in the play [18]Macbeth asserts that *time and the hour run through the roughest day,* now Malcolm looks forward to a new dawn when he declares that *the night is long that never finds the day.*

Act 5 Scene 1

We now see that Lady Macbeth's mental health has deteriorated to such an extent that she is re-enacting the night of Duncan's murder in her sleep. The gentlewoman refuses to tell the doctor what she has heard Lady Macbeth say, despite his insistence*: 'Tis most meet you should.* As the scene proceeds and we hear Lady Macbeth's words, we realise that the gentlewoman is afraid of being accused of treason, and therefore needs a witness.

The constant washing her hands action mocks Lady Macbeth's words to her husband on the night of the murder:

A little water clears us of this deed.
How easy is it then![19]

The gentlewoman tells the doctor that Lady Macbeth has a light by her constantly, revealing the terror of darkness, a darkness that had once been embraced. Lady Macbeth's *Hell is murky* contrasts strongly with her invitation to *thick night* in an earlier scene[20] and wishing for *the blanket of the dark* to hide the sight of murder.

The woman who talked, without revulsion or fear, of smearing the grooms with Duncan's blood, now laments, *Yet who would have thought the old man to have so much*

---

[18] Act 1 Scene 3
[19] Act 2 Scene 2
[20] Act 1 Scene 5

blood in him. She wonders further what has happened to Lady Macduff, perhaps telling us that she no longer has access to her husband's thoughts, plans and actions, that there has been breakdown of a relationship which was so close that he wrote to her on his way back from battle, calling her, his *dearest partner of greatness.*[21]

Lady Macbeth, fast asleep, imagines she can smell Duncan's blood, and in anguish, cries, *All the perfumes of Arabia will not sweeten this little hand,* contrasting with Macbeth's anguish on the night of the murder:

Will all great Neptune's ocean wash this blood
Clean from my hand?[22]

He knows that nothing will metaphorically cleanse him, and follows this cry with a despairing:

No. This my hand will rather
The multitudinous seas incarnadine,
Making the green one red.

It is not only the murders of Duncan and Lady Macduff that are preying on Lady Macbeth's mind, but also that of Banquo. She re-lives her reassurance to Macbeth that Banquo was *buried; he cannot come out on's grave.*

With her repetition of the words *to bed, to bed, to bed* Lady Macbeth now takes herself back to bed, leaving the doctor commenting that it was the *divine* not the *physician* that she needs. He realises that she is possibly suicidal and urges the gentlewoman to remove anything that she could harm herself with, and both of them are left disturbed by what they have witnessed.

---

[21] Act 1 Scene 5
[22] Act 2 Scene 2

Act 5 Scene 2

The remaining scenes are a kaleidoscope, constantly shifting from the situation and perspective of Macbeth, with the deterioration of his mental and emotional state, to that of the English army, Malcolm and Macduff, as they draw ever closer to Dunsinane. In this scene, four of the nobles discuss the situation as it now stands. We learn the *English power* and the leaders are burning with desire for revenge. Malcolm has lost a father, Macduff, wife and children, and Siward is called Uncle by Malcolm, as Shakespeare mixes fact and fiction freely. All are united in their aim to free Scotland from the tyranny of Macbeth and place Malcolm on the throne.

When Angus declares that the Scots will meet them *near Birnam Wood* we are immediately reminded of the witches' prophecy that Macbeth cannot be defeated until Birnam Wood should come to Dunsinane. Donalbain has not yet returned from Ireland and the English army is bolstered with many young men fighting for the first time, including Siward's son.

Caithness reveals that Macbeth is fortifying his castle at Dunsinane and there are various opinions of his state of mind. While some assert that he is mad, others say he is consumed by a warlike rage. What is certain is that he cannot use the fact that he is king to justify his actions.

In reply Angus considers that Macbeth must feel *his secret murders sticking on his hands* and is having to face new rebellions every minute. Those who are fighting for him are obeying orders only, not acting from love. The title of king must feel very loose, *like a giant's robe upon a dwarfish thief.*

Menteith shrewdly comments that Macbeth must be feeling very agitated as he must be condemning himself, and Caithness concludes that they are marching on to obey the rightful king, Malcolm, who will purge the country.

Act 5 Scene 3

The focus shifts back to Macbeth in Dunsinane Castle. He freely speaks of what he is feeling despite attendants and the doctor being present. Desperately holding on to the witches' words, Macbeth dismisses the troubling reports he is hearing about rebellion and desertion with a defiant,

> *'Till Birnam Wood remove to Dunsinane,*
> *I cannot taint with fear*

His words are powerful, declaring that his heart *shall never sag with doubt, nor shake with fear.*

However, we realise how disturbed and close to the edge he has come when he turns on a servant and abuses him cruelly: *The devil damn thee black, thou cream-faced loon.* The news the servant brings, that ten thousand English soldiers are approaching, contributes to his feeling *sick at heart* as he knows that the English attack will be the deciding factor. He muses sorrowfully that his life has become like a dry, yellow leaf, and uses the word *sear* to describe the burning or scarring he has endured. He reflects that the good things of old age such as *honour, love, obedience, troops of friends*, will not be his, for his lot will be to receive silent curses, insincere flattery and lip-service.[23]

Still his resolve is not diminished, and hearing that the servant's report is accurate, he is determined to *fight till from my bones my flesh be hacked.* Belatedly turning to the doctor, he finally asks how his wife is faring and the doctor gives a discreet reply saying that she is physically well but her mind cannot rest. Clearly, the doctor cannot say what Lady Macbeth has inadvertently revealed.

Macbeth's appeal to the doctor, which follows, applies to himself equally. This is a profoundly poignant speech, and comes from the heart. He cannot expect the doctor to

---

[23] Further analysis page 49

have a cure for *a mind diseased* or *the written troubles of the brain*, but with such longing he pleads for *a sweet oblivious antidote to* cleanse the heart of the dangerous thoughts that fill it. [24]

Perhaps the doctor is confused by such a request but his answer is brusque in that the patient must cure himself, and Macbeth throws off his pondering to dismiss medicine and ironically tell the doctor that he would applaud him *to the echo* if he could find a cure for the country, and find some *purgative drug* to rid him of the English army.[25]

There is black humour when Macbeth asks the doctor if he had heard of the English invasion, and the doctor dryly returns, *Your royal preparation makes us hear something,* and mutters to himself that no matter what he was offered if he could get away from Dunsinane he would not return.

Act 5 Scene 4

The attacking armies are now combined and Malcolm is rallying the soldiers. Finding that the wood near them is Birnam, he commands every soldier to cut down a bough to bear before him, so as to disguise the numbers, making the witches' prophecy even more of a threat. Malcolm comments on the fact that Macbeth has decided on a siege, saying that it is his best hope as so many have deserted him. Only those forced to do so are staying to fight.

Macduff says they still have to fight hard and well, while Siward finishes the comments with the fact that speculation has no part, for only fighting would provide the answer.

Act 5 Scene 5

This scene returns to the castle and Macbeth with his mixture of defiance and despair. The soldier vies with the poet, the man of fearful, annihilistic imagination. He knows

---

[24] Further analysis page 48

[25] Further analysis page 48

his castle is secure and that he could *laugh a siege to scorn.* Starvation and fever would defeat the besiegers. If the oncoming army were not reinforced with deserters from Macbeth's army he could have beaten it.

The cry of women causes him to remember that there was a time when his senses would have *cooled* to hear such a *night-shriek* and that a frightening story would have made his hair stand on end. Seyton returns to tell him that Lady Macbeth is dead, and his response is shocking for a man who has appeared so devoted to his wife earlier in the play. There are two interpretations for his words:

She should have died hereafter;
There would have been time for such a word.

One is that she had to die sometime, but a far more likely reason is that although he has become a monster, Macbeth would not have dismissed her death so summarily, and thinks that his wife should have died at a later time as his present circumstances leave him no time to mourn.

His despair and sense of resignation now become almost tangible as he reflects on the futility of life which *creeps* on to the end of the world. The past is proof of the fact that we are *fools* who live a life of illusion which leads to a *dusty death.* Life is unreal, and human beings are like actors who play out their time on the stage and are then silenced by death. Life is a story told by an idiot, full of noise and passion, and it is totally meaningless. [26]

A messenger arrives to tell him that he has seen Birnam Wood moving towards the castle, and Macbeth's anxiety overflows: *liar and slave,* and warns the messenger that if he is lying *upon the next tree shalt thou hang alive till famine cling thee.* There is a sense of resignation in his added remark that if the messenger's words are true he doesn't care if the same fate is inflicted on himself.

---

[26] Further analysis of this speech page 49

Macbeth now begins to doubt, rather late in the day, whether the witches were being truthful; he begins to *pull in resolution* for his certainty is shaken. He calls the witches' words *th' equivocation of the fiend,* and we remember the porter's words on equivocation where truth and lies become confused, and *now a wood comes towards Dunsinane*. He knows that his situation is impossible and it is impossible to escape or stay. His *I 'gin to be a-weary of the sun* is despairing as he wishes the world would fall apart, a very different mood, however, from the Macbeth who boldly told the witches even if *destruction sicken* and the world fell apart, he would have answers, as he defiantly struggled to keep his kingship.[27] But then that defiance then flares into action once more as he vows to die fighting: *At least we'll die with harness on our back.*

Act 5 Scene 6

Malcolm decides on the battle plan with Siward and his son, young Siward, leading the first battle, and Malcolm and Macduff doing what else remains to be done. Siward expresses determination:

Do we but find the tyrant's power tonight,
Let us be beaten, if we cannot fight.

Macduff orders the trumpets, *those clamorous harbingers of blood and death* to *speak.*

Act 5 Scene 7

Macbeth feels like a bear *tied to a stake* and knows he must fight. He attempts to reassure himself that no one *born of woman* needs to be feared.

He encounters young Siward who fights bravely but Macbeth kills him, triumphantly declaring that he cannot be

[27] Act 4 Scene 1

hurt by weapons *brandished by man that's of a woman born.*

Meanwhile Macduff is looking for Macbeth. He is interested in fighting no one else especially hired foot soldiers. He hears sounds of fighting and pleads:

Let me find him Fortune,
And more I beg not.

Siward announces that Macbeth's castle gave up with little resistance, and that the *tyrant's people* were fighting on both sides. The day is as good as won. Malcolm confirms that they have met *foes* who changed sides to fight with them.

Macbeth appears as they exit, defiantly asking himself why he should *play the Roman fool and die on mine own sword?* an allusion to the tradition that Roman generals committed suicide when the battle seemed lost, rather than be captured. The wounds would be better inflicted upon his enemies than on himself.

It is at that moment that Macduff finds Macbeth, triumphantly ordering, *Turn hell-hound turn!*

It is interesting to note that at this stage in the play when Macbeth appears to have become increasingly immune to conscience, clothed in brutality, lashing out at all who oppose him, abusing servants and messengers, all vestiges of compassion gone, that he finds it within himself to feel remorse at what he had done to Macduff's family. His words: *My soul is too much charg'd with blood of thine already* come from the heart, causing us to wonder how much he has suffered emotionally for his actions, and what has been his state of mind as he has ruthlessly gone down the path of destroying any opposition. Once his ambitions of kingship were achieved and he had committed the worst sin it was thought possible to commit, the murder of God's deputy, there was no way back, just an iron determination to hold on to what he had, and we recall his fear that *For Banquo's issue have I 'filed my mind:*

For them the gracious Duncan have I murdered.[28]

He has sold his soul to the devil and after such an experience he will fight with every fibre of his being to hold on to what he has gained so brutally.

His courage cannot be faulted as he fights Macduff, but he believes at this juncture that he is safe, telling Macduff that he was wasting his time as he cannot be defeated by *one of woman born*. But Macduff *was from his mother's womb untimely ripped* probably a very primitive form of a caesarean birth, and Macbeth finally realises that the witches had been playing games with him, yet more equivocation in this play.

He admits that it has *cowed* him to hear Macduff's words, and curses him for the knowledge. Calling the witches *juggling fiends* Macbeth says they *palter with us in a double sense* once more bringing up the theme of equivocation. The realisation is now cemented that he has been fooled, despite suspecting it before, [29]when he had begun to *doubt the equivocation of the fiend that lies like truth.* Despair takes over and he tells Macduff, *I'll not fight with thee*.

Macduff taunts him with cowardice, assuring him that he will be made a public spectacle for all to see, and once more an accusation of cowardice [30]rallies him to fight. His words are defiant:

I will not yield
To kiss the ground before young Malcolm's feet,
And to be baited with the rabble's curse.

Even though the witches' prophecies have come true in a way that is disastrous for him, Macbeth will now fight to the end. We can only surmise that despite this last act of

---

[28] Act 3 Scene 1
[29] Act 5 Scene 6
[30] Lady Macbeth Act 1 Scene 7

courage he knew that he was doomed even as he utters his final words:

Lay on, Macduff,
And damned be him that first cries 'Hold, enough!'

Act 5 Scene 8

In this final scene everything is brought together and the rightful heir to the throne is triumphant. Law and order are restored. There have been few lives lost on Malcolm's side, and Siward takes the news of the death of his son, philosophically, saying that had he as many sons as he had hairs *I would not wish them to a fairer death.* Malcolm reacts quite sharply to this attitude, saying,

He's worth more sorrow,
And that I'll spend for him.

The stoical Siward insists *He's worth no more,* and we are reminded of Roman mothers who would tell their war bound sons not to come back if they had wounds in their backs.

Macduff enters victoriously, holding aloft Macbeth's head, and urges everyone to join in with him to celebrate Malcolm as the monarch: *Hail, King of Scotland.*

Malcolm's final speech is reminiscent of Duncan's generosity and appreciation of others. Slipping into the royal *we* he tells his listeners that he intends to *reckon with your several loves*, and alongside these rewards will be new titles, earls. Exiled friends, fleeing from Macbeth's tyranny, would be welcomed home again to a free Scotland, and all that is necessary for him to do would be done carefully and conscientiously. All are invited to Scone for his coronation.

Part 2 Analysis and Explanation

1 Soliloquies

Soliloquies are used by the playwright to enlighten the audience about characters' innermost, true feelings: as they are musing aloud to themselves, we assume that this is being done honestly.

a. *If it were done…*

In this soliloquy Shakespeare plays with words when Macbeth entertains the hope that if the murder could be over and done with, without any repercussions, then *t'were well it were done quickly*. The repetition of *done* reveals the anxiety Macbeth is feeling about the regicide so keenly urged by his wife.

A Jacobean audience would have been shocked by the idea of a man taking his chances with eternal judgement in order to fulfil an earthly ambition, yet that is exactly what Macbeth asserts: *here upon this bank and shoal of time we'd jump the life to come.* Thus for a brief span of life as king, Macbeth is willing to risk an eternity of hell. Later, this is bitterly regretted when he laments that for Banquo's children he has given his *eternal jewel* to *the common enemy of man,* the devil. After the murder of Duncan, Macbeth is terrified because he could not echo the prayers of Malcolm and Donalbain. He says, *I had most need of blessing and Amen stuck in my throat.*[31]

After his apparent defiance of judgement in an afterworld, Macbeth begins to think again. He muses that there is judgement on earth to face and what we do will come back to punish us: *we but teach bloody instructions, which being taught return to plague the inventor.*

[31] Act 2 Scene 2

Colloquially, we could translate that as 'what goes around, comes around.' Justice is *even-handed* and the contents of the *poisoned chalice* should be drunk by the perpetrator. Although a chalice is a large wine glass or goblet it is also used for communion wine, a Christian service in which symbolically the wine is the blood of Christ, so there is something oxymoronic about a poisoned chalice, highlighting the sinfulness of the act of murder.

Macbeth moves on to consider other reasons why he should not kill Duncan. The king was his cousin, he was the king's subject, and these factors are *both strong against the deed.* Macbeth was also Duncan's host and should be protecting him, not murdering him. Then he launches into a litany of praise about Duncan's virtues, who is *so clear in his great office* that there will be a general outcry of outrage and pity with the wind *blowing the horrid deed in every eye.*

Finally, Macbeth admits that he has no *spur* or motivation to *prick the sides of my intent* save *vaulting ambition* which he realises will prove to be his downfall. At this stage Macbeth has weighed up the situation accurately and he realises that no good can come from murdering the king, and decided against proceeding further with the murder.

b. Is this a dagger which I see before me? Act 2 Scene 1

This will not be the only time that Macbeth hallucinates in this play: indeed the next time will be far more terrifying, when he believes that he sees Banquo's ghost. He also has awareness of the fact that this time the pressure of the situation is affecting him, a consolation which will elude him where Banquo's ghost is concerned, for by then he will be incapable of believing. But now:

It is the bloody business which informs
Thus to mine eyes.

The plosive alliteration highlights the intensity of his emotions.

He tries to grip the dagger but finds cannot, and he addresses the dagger as if it could understand, asking it if was able to be touched as well as seen. He begins to question its authenticity when he asks if it is a *false creation* arising from his fevered brain. Despite this suspicion he continues trying to prove the dagger is real: *in form as palpable* as his own dagger which he draws in evidence, observing that the dagger is now moving in the direction of Duncan's room. He ponders on the fact that either his eyes or his other senses are lying to each other, for he now sees drops of blood on the blade and handle.

Macbeth pulls himself together, realising that his nerves and senses are taut and at breaking point, and that he is imagining the dagger. He muses on the fact that night is appropriate for murder, while *wicked dreams abuse the curtained sleep.* The word *curtained* has more than one connotation: literally, the curtains round the bed of the wealthier classes to exclude draughts, and the eyelids.

Night is a time for witches to *celebrate pale Hecate's offerings*, and as Hecate was goddess of the moon as well as witchcraft, *pale* would recognise the moon's pastel shade. *Withered murder* is moving stealthily towards his victim, just as Tarquinius, the son of a Roman ruler moved towards the room of the wife of a Roman noble where he raped her. This evil stealth links in with Macbeth's stealthy approach towards Duncan's room.

He asks the earth not to hear his footsteps, in case the rattle of stones gives him away, and will therefore break the horrifying atmosphere so necessary to his plans, concluding that too much talking will reduce his desire to act.

A rhyming triplet brings the soliloquy and scene to an end, and Macbeth addresses the sleeping Duncan directly, telling him that his funeral bell (knell) is summoning him *to heaven or to hell.*

c. *Banquo's soliloquy Act 3 Scene 1*

Thou hast it now, king, Cawdor, Glamis, all…

Banquo makes clear what we have suspected already, that he realises that Macbeth murdered Duncan. The proof that he would never have been complicit in such an act is in, *I fear thou playd'st most foully for it,* yet we observe that he has done nothing about it, which is puzzling and makes us doubt his integrity, even more so when we discover why he hasn't acted, or sought the vengeance that Macduff pursues from the outset.

The reason he hasn't acted is revealed when Banquo muses on the fact that it had been predicted that it was his children who would benefit. It was he who would be *the root and father of many kings*, and we are reminded of the night of the murder when he tells Fleance that he does not want to sleep despite his exhaustion for fear of the thoughts that came to him when he was resting. When Macbeth enters Banquo tells him that he had dreamed of the witches, commenting *to you they have showed some truth.*

Banquo continues to ponder that as they had predicted *verities* (truths) *on thee made good* they might prove to be his *oracles* as well, and we understand all too well the reason for his silence. His ambition is laid bare and he articulates his hopes.

d. *To be thus, is nothing, but to be safely thus Act 3 Scene 1*

Macbeth has had time to brood over Banquo, and his fears are twofold: the suspicions Banquo must have of him and the fact that the witches have prophesied that it will be Banquo's heirs who will be the future kings of Scotland.

We learn that Macbeth fears Banquo's *royalty of nature*, an allusion to Banquo having the qualities of kingship, a fact that would remind Macbeth of Banquo being told *thou shalt get kings*[32]. Perhaps we can assume that it is the prophecy rather than anything else that has put the observation of Banquo having such a noble nature into Macbeth's mind, and also fear. Indeed, earlier in the play, it is Macbeth who has been given the plaudits of nobility, although Duncan does admit that Banquo is *noble* and *hast no less deserved.*[33] Even so it is Macbeth who receives the reward of Thane of Cawdor, and this is just a preliminary gift, as Angus comments that he and Ross have been sent by Duncan *only to herald thee into his sight, not pay thee.*

Macbeth pays tribute to Banquo's *dauntless* (brave) nature and his *wisdom* that guides his exploits safely, and comes to the conclusion once more that he fears no one else but Banquo. Why should Macbeth fear Banquo? He maintains that Banquo curbs his spirit or *genius* and likens this holding back to the manner in which Octavius Caesar restrained Mark Antony's spirit. However, we see no real evidence of this restraint in the play, except for Banquo advising Macbeth about the trickery of *instruments of darkness* when the witches prophecy such high honour for Macbeth, and the fact that he did indeed chide the witches, telling them that he cares not whether they *favour* him or *hate* him.[34]

It is probable that the fear Macbeth suffers is the realisation that Banquo must be aware that he is Duncan's murderer. Only a few hours before Duncan's body is found Macbeth has urged Banquo to take his advice when they next talk. Banquo's reply is firm in that he says that will do so as long as can keep his conscience and *allegiance clear.* It would seem that he suspects something treasonable is being suggested, and wants no part of it.

Macbeth then reflects upon the predictions made for Banquo and his heirs, and that he is left with *a fruitless crown* and *barren sceptre.* The alliterative *no son of mine*

---

[32] Act 1 Scene 3
[33] Act 1 Scene 4
[34] Act 1 Scene 3

succeeding has a bitter ring to the words, and there is anguish in the lines that follow as he ponders on the fact that he has murdered *the gracious Duncan* for Banquo's heirs, has filled his mind with bitterness and given his *eternal jewel* to *the common enemy of man.* This sacrifice of his soul to the devil is reminiscent of Faustus and his pact with Lucifer.[35] Macbeth rallies at the end of the soliloquy, and determines that rather than the predictions should come true concerning Banquo, he will fight Fate in deadly combat.

2. Four speeches in Act 5, which reveal Macbeth's state of mind and increasing despair.

a Act 5 Scene 3

I have lived long enough...

Macbeth has just learned that ten thousand soldiers are advancing on Dunsinane. His feelings are expressed in anger which subsides into despair as he reflects on what is left to him, how he can only look forward to condemnation and isolation from all that he could have enjoyed in old age, such as *honour, love, obedience, troops of friends* which are now denied him. At the beginning of the play, before we met him in the third scene, this was the man who was praised and venerated; Duncan calls him, *valiant cousin, worthy gentleman!* and also terms him *noble*. In Scene 4, when the two men come face to face, Duncan tells his cousin that *more is thy due than more than all* can *pay.* All these plaudits are distant memories as Macbeth can now only anticipate *curses, not loud but deep, mouth-honour* from those afraid to condemn him openly.

[35] Dr. Faustus Christopher Marlowe

b. Act 5 Scene 3

Canst thou not minister to a mind diseased…

Here, Macbeth asks the doctor, with no real hope, if he can cure someone who is deeply, emotionally troubled. Ostensibly he is talking about his wife but he too is suffering and his words are anguished. He is seeking a *sweet oblivious antidote* to clear his wife's heart of the dangerous or *perilous* thoughts which are destroying her, but the *rooted sorrow* and *written troubles of the brain* could well apply to him also.

c. Act 5 Scene 3

If thou couldst, doctor, cast the water of my land…

Again, Macbeth is pondering on cures, this time for a diseased Scotland, when ironically, it is he who has caused the sickness. He wishes Scotland could be *purged,* a powerful word with connotations of a total eradication of the damage which he has caused. He asks if the doctor could *cast the water*, referring to the practice of testing a patient's urine to find the cause of an illness. His words are heartfelt when he tells the doctor that if he could return Scotland to *a sound and pristine health* he would applaud the doctor *to the very echo, that should applaud again.*

Then, abruptly, Macbeth asks *'what rhubarb, senna or what purgative drug* would get rid of the English? The sickness metaphors in these musings are indicative of how he surely realises that his ambition has brought a nation to a parlous state, in which another country has become involved in order to remove the destructive, evil force which is controlling it. Scotland is indeed sick, and Macduff has previously lamented:

Each new morn
New widows howl, new orphans cry, new sorrows
Strike heaven on the face.[36]

---

[36] Act 4 Scene 3

d. Act 5 Scene 5

She should have died hereafter...

Macbeth has learned of his wife's death and ponders that she should have died at a later time when he would have had time to mourn. Another interpretation is that Lady Macbeth had to die sometime, but it is difficult to think of him dismissing her death so casually.

The annihilistic words that follow, mirror Macbeth's increasing despair. Life is futile; its *petty pace* creeps on relentlessly until the end of the world: *the last syllable of recorded time*. The past demonstrates this as *fools* have made their way to *dusty death*. Life is unreal, *a walking shadow,* a man is like an actor who has his *hour upon the stage,* working his way through both the good and stressful times in life, and then after all his furious struggle, he dies and can strive no more. The words *fools* and *idiot* are indicative of the credulity and pointlessness of the human life.

The use of harsh and plosive alliteration in *petty pace* and *dusty death* emphasise Macbeth's disillusion and despair.

e. Act 3 Scene 2

Two speeches ~ husband and wife have similar thoughts

We hear Lady Macbeth's thoughts for the first time since the murder and discover that she is feeling deeply disturbed. Her words make this very clear.

Naught's had, all's spent,
Where our desire is got without content.
'Tis safer to be that which we destroy,
Than by destruction dwell in doubtful joy.

Lady Macbeth here bewails the utter futility of achieving what is desired when it brings no happiness. Her words shock as she now believes that it would be more desirable to be murdered than to murder, a striking change of heart from the woman we have previously encountered.

However, we see a striking change in her attitude when Macbeth enters. She pulls herself together and strives to raise his mood. She tells him that his *sorriest fancies* should have died with Duncan, and that he shouldn't be brooding on things that cannot be changed: *what's done is done*, words that will return to haunt her in the sleepwalking scene: *What's done cannot be undone.*

There is no cheering Macbeth. He is fearful. He uses a metaphor of a wounded snake that will heal and lash out to explain the danger he thinks is ahead. He describes *terrible dreams* that rack him every night, and then we hear him echo the words that Lady Macbeth spoke in solitude:

Better be with the dead,
Whom we, to gain our peace, have sent to peace,
Than on the torture of the mind to lie
In restless ecstasy.

Thus, he has no compunction in telling her about his frantic, sleepless state of mind, while she has hidden her own anguish in trying to cheer him.

Macbeth continues by appearing to be envious of Duncan, sleeping peacefully in his grave: treason, murder, civil war, foreign invasion are all things that can touch him no longer.

3. Characters

a. Duncan ~ the Concept of Kingship

In this play we see portraits of two ideal kings, and one ruthless, tyrannical king, juxtaposed.

We never hear anything derogatory said about Duncan who is portrayed as gracious, courteous and generous. He is quick to praise, acknowledging the value of Macbeth's success and his own inability to ever repay him sufficiently: *More is thy due than more than all can pay.*[37]

There is a certain irony in Duncan's naïve trust in others as he comments on the Thane of Cawdor:

there's no art
To find the mind's construction in the face,

as his trust in him had been *absolute.*

That Thane of Cawdor betrayed him; the next Thane of Cawdor, whom he also trusts, will murder him.

Macbeth glibly reminds Duncan that the king's part is solely to receive the *duties* which his subjects owe him, further irony.

Duncan, happy after the day's successes promises rewards for *all deservers* after proclaiming that Malcolm would be his heir. The system of primogeniture, the handing down of title and property to the eldest son, was not in force in eleventh century Scotland, so perhaps Macbeth had hoped that Duncan would choose him as his heir:

If chance will have me king,
Why chance may crown me,
[38]*Without my stir.*

---

[37] Act 1 Scene 4
[38] Act 1 Scene 3

Again, we see a gracious Duncan when he addresses Lady Macbeth as *honoured hostess*[39] and shows concern for the trouble his visit might give, promising to reward her. Duncan comments, regarding Macbeth,' We love him highly', and assures her that he will continue his 'graces towards him'.[40]Later Duncan sends a diamond to his 'most kind hostess' and money to the servants.

Macbeth never attempts to justify the murder of Duncan but considers that he has been such a great king that the supernatural will become involved:

his virtues
Will plead like angels, trumpet-tongued against
The deep damnation of his taking-off.[41]

There will be so much pity aroused that *tears shall drown the wind.*

Banquo tells Macbeth that he will listen to any advice that he wishes to give as long as he can keep his *bosom franchised, and allegiance clear'*,[42] thus stating quite firmly that his duty is towards the king.

Macduff's appalled outburst reminds us that the king was considered God's appointment, and that his body was a temple:

Most sacrilegious murder hath broke ope
The Lord's anointed temple, and stole thence
The life of the building.[43]

The theme of the king being above normal human beings, is continued with the description of nature being thrown into confusion with his murder. Lennox talks of the strange

---

[39] Act 1 Scene 6
[40] Act 1 Scene 5
[41] Act 1 Scene 7
[42] Act 2 Scene 1
[43] Act 2 Scene 3

events of the night with storms, voices and an earthquake, while a conversation between Ross and an old man reveals that Duncan's horses ate each other. A mousing owl had attacked a falcon and killed it, which could almost be a metaphor for someone below the king in stature murdering him.

Macbeth refers to Duncan as *gracious* when he reflects upon the fact that he has possibly murdered him for Banquo's descendants, and mourns the fact that he will have *a fruitless crown*, a *barren sceptre*, both to be *wrenched* from him by an *unlineal hand.*[44]

In the Pit of Acheron scene, Macbeth comments on the fact that some of the kings in the line carried *twofold balls and treble sceptres,* [45]an allusion to the fact that James 1 ruled both England and Scotland.

Malcolm demonstrates that he will not be as naïve and trusting as his father when he tests Macduff's integrity and validity. Carolyn Asp has described Malcolm as *a subdued, more Machiavellian version of Duncan.* [46]It is true that Malcolm displays none of the overt emotion of his father, but is quick to promise rewards as Duncan did before him.

In the Malcolm/Macduff scene we learn of the spiritual gifts of Edward the Confessor, and see the tremendous chasm between the nature of the English king and the current Scottish one. Edward functions in the light: Macbeth in the dark, both literally and metaphorically. The English king is a long way from the instruments of darkness. He *solicits heaven* unlike the hell that Macbeth seeks. There is a compliment to James 1 in this scene also, as Malcolm informs Macduff that *to the succeeding royalty he leaves the healing benediction.*[47]

---

[44] Act 3 Scene 1

[45] Act 4 Scene 1

[46] Carolyn Asp 'Tragic Action and Sexual Stereotyping in 'Macbeth'.

[47] Act 4 Scene 3

b. Macbeth as a Tragic Hero

Aristotle maintained that there was a certain pleasure to be gained from tragedy in drama, but qualified this by calling it a *proper pleasure* which is a catharsis of pity and fear which shows a good man *passing by a series of probable or necessary stages...from happiness to misfortune.*[48]

For Aristotle catharsis is purification or cleansing, a release of emotional tension. This comes as a result of anagnorisis, a moment of tragic recognition in which the protagonist realises some important fact or insight, especially a truth about himself, human nature or his situation.

A tragic hero, according to tradition, had to be of royal or noble birth and be of high reputation in the community in which he lived. However, he (and Shakespeare's four major tragedies all have male heroes) also has a fatal flaw which will bring about his downfall and death. Thus, Hamlet's procrastination, Lear's pride, Othello's jealousy and Macbeth's *vaulting ambition* all cause their possessors' deaths, although it is debatable to what extent each deserves it.

Macbeth was of royal birth as he was the king's cousin. He was also Thane of Glamis when the play opens, as he has inherited the title from his father, Sinel. After his bravery and exploits on the battlefield Duncan confers the title of Thane of Cawdor on him, calling him *valiant cousin, worthy gentleman*! [49]Later, when Macbeth joins Duncan, probably at Forres, although it is not stated, Duncan confesses that Macbeth has done so much for him that it was impossible to repay him quickly enough. On the night of the murder of the king, Macbeth is reluctant to lose the *golden opinions*[50] so many people have of him. Thus, he is

---

[48] Aristotle Poetics

[49] Act 1 Scene 2

[50] Act 1 Scene 7

of very high reputation in the community. His fatal flaw, his boundless ambition, will not only bring about his own downfall, and his wife's suicide, but will destroy many others who are innocent. However, the tragic hero's death is necessary to re establish law, order and morality, once more.

Macbeth's ambition makes him vulnerable to the predictions of the witches, despite Banquo's warnings about the evil seduction of the *instruments of darkness.* [51] He lusts for power, and is prepared to murder in order to achieve it, but his vivid imagination causes him torment after murdering Duncan and Banquo. However, he becomes hardened and declares that his acts *want hard use* for he is *but young in deed.*[52]

c. *Lady Macbeth, the ruthless persuader*

We first meet Lady Macbeth in Act 1 Scene 5. By this time we are very aware of how esteemed and popular Macbeth is, and how much Duncan owes to him for defeating his enemies.

In Scene 5 Lady Macbeth is reading a letter from Macbeth, in which she learns about his encounter with the witches, and what they have promised. Her reaction is immediate and delighted:

> *Glamis thou art, and Cawdor, and shalt be what thou art promised.*

However, she fears that he isn't ruthless enough to carry out the murder of Duncan, that he is:

---

[51] Act 1 Scene 3

[52] Act 3 Scene 4

Too full of the milk of human kindness to catch the nearest way.

Here she is referring to his compassion (although we never see any demonstrated by him in the play) and *the nearest way* alludes to murder which would be the quickest and surest way for Macbeth to achieve the throne. It is interesting to note that Lady Macbeth's first thought on receiving the letter was the murder of Duncan, and suggests that she and Macbeth had discussed the possibility previously.

At this stage we also learn that she has tremendous influence over her husband as she goes on to urge his speedy return home that:

I may pour my spirits in thine ear, and chastise with the valour of my tongue

all that might prevent him from gaining the throne. *Valour* here has connotations of power and persuasion.

We see further evidence of her power over her husband in subsequent scenes, an unusual event for Jacobean England, when women were expected to be submissive and gentle, controlled by their husbands, and considered to be intellectually inferior. They were also considered to be unable to bear anything fearful or deeply unpleasant and would need the protection of men. Thus, Macduff says after he discovers the body of Duncan:

O gentle lady, 'tis not for you to hear what I can speak
The repetition in a woman's ear, would murder as it fell.

This comment is ironic of course, as he is talking to the woman who has planned the terrible deed.

But an interesting initial sign of Lady Macbeth's weakness is when she realises that although her desire and determination are strong, she fears that she might not be strong enough to carry out her evil intentions. Therefore, she calls on evil spirits to help her and to make her *top-full of direst cruelty.* She wants remorse prevented, her milk changed to a bitter substance called gall, and hell involved in blocking heaven from observing what is happening and so stopping the murder.

Lady Macbeth's first words to her husband when he returns from battle are not concern for his wellbeing, but an affirmation of his future as king:

Great Glamis, worthy Cawdor,
Greater than both by the all-hail hereafter.

She warns Macbeth that his face *is as a book* so it is possible to see what he is thinking, and that he must be more deceptive in the way he looks and acts. She tells her husband to leave all the arrangements for *this night's great business* to her and it will lead to kingship and *masterdom.* She insists that he must behave normally and states firmly, *Leave all the rest to me.*

When Duncan arrives at the castle in Inverness, Lady Macbeth greets him with all the submissive respect that would be expected of her. Her attitude and tone bear no relation to the fierce, determined woman we have previously seen. She is a dangerous, deceptive woman, hell bent on achieving the kingship for her husband.

Act 2

Macbeth leaves the feast to be on his own and soliloquise about murdering Duncan, quickly coming to the conclusion that Duncan is a great king, and that all he has in his favour is *vaulting ambition.*

Lady Macbeth comes to find him and has a powerful reaction to the news that her husband wishes to *proceed no further in this business,* and accuses him of cowardice, and of being drunk when he first proposed the murder of Duncan. This accusation is interesting as we have not seen Macbeth suggest the murder to his wife, thus we can infer that such a conversation took place in the past. Lady Macbeth also uses emotional blackmail, telling her husband that from that moment *such I account thy love,* and she taunts him with the fact that he would always know that he was a coward, afraid to murder, although wanting the crown, like a cat who wanted fish but was afraid to dip his paws into a pond and get them wet.

She knows her husband well, and his reaction to accusations of cowardice is one of anger:

Prithee, peace! I dare do all that may become a man, who dares do more is none.

Lady Macbeth has not finished. She continues to insult his masculinity, something very hard for this man of action to take, and also refers again to what might well have been an earlier conversation on the subject, when she says that previously he was willing to find place and opportunity even though neither was available. Then she says something shocking, that if she had broken such a vow as he intends to do, she would have taken a baby while feeding it, and *dashed the brains out.* He begins to submit to her wishes, and then she also explains how she will drug Duncan's guards, and the *spongy officers* can be blamed for the murder.

Macbeth does not react with shock, but instead admiration, for the masculine qualities she is displaying, urging her to *bring forth male children only.* Her powerful persuasion has overcome all his doubts and scruples and he is now determined to see the evil deed through to its conclusion, again declaring the intention to put on a *false face* to hide his *false heart.*

As she concludes her preparations for the murder we see an anxious, jittery Lady Macbeth, another sign of the weakness that she tries to suppress. She says that she could have murdered Duncan herself if it wasn't for the fact that he looked so like her father as he slept. She hears an owl shriek and that startles her also. She terms the bird *the fatal bellman*, an allusion to the bell rung outside the cell of a condemned man the night before execution.

When Macbeth calls out to her she is afraid, again thinking they have been caught in the act, not realising at that moment that it is her husband.

Husband and wife then indulge in the quick exchange of words termed stichomythia, displaying their agitation, but Lady Macbeth pulls herself together quickly, having little patience with Macbeth's stark fear of what he has done and how it has alienated him from God (hardly surprising when he has murdered God's deputy). He is filled with remorse and her response is brutal, *Infirm of purpose* and tells him he is thinking *brainsickly.* She sees things very simply, that water will clean the blood from their hands, *how easy is it then.* She has no understanding of his mental torture and conscience, and Shakespeare paints her as a ruthless, inflexible woman, lacking imagination and conscience. But her inflexibility will prove to be her undoing because what cannot bend, must break when the pressure is too great. She devotes her life to supporting her husband, her ambitions are all for him, and when this begins to unravel, when she is no longer his confidante, her purpose in life disappears.

Lady Macbeth's sense of what is appropriate in certain situations also deserts her when she learns of Duncan's murder. Her *What in our house?* receives a stern rebuke from Banquo, and later, when Macbeth's hyperbolic speech about why he killed the guards might arouse suspicion, she takes refuge in fainting. This could have been genuine and another sign of weakness, but it could have been a diversionary tactic to protect her husband from saying anything else which might prove dangerous for him.

Act 3

Lady Macbeth is no longer happy. Why she has changed her attitude is not altogether clear, except it is very apparent that what the two of them have achieved has brought her no satisfaction.

She comments that nothing has been gained, everything wasted, and that '*tis safer to be that which we destroy, than by destruction dwell in doubtful joy.* This comes as a shock to the audience for she has changed from single minded ruthlessness to regret about their actions, even feeling that she would be better off dead than living in such unhappiness.

What is particularly interesting about this is that as soon as Macbeth joins her she urges him to forget what they have done, for if nothing can be done about a situation then it should be forgotten. *What's done is done,* she insists, in marked reversal to what she has said when alone.

Then Macbeth, who does not seem to feel his wife needs protecting in the same way that she protects him, pours out his feelings, and they are virtually identical to the ones we have just observed her reveal: *Better be with the dead, whom we to gain our peace have sent to peace.*

Once again, we see a wife, ambitious for her husband, but also fiercely protective of his mental state, hide her own feelings in order to cheer him. He hints that he has plans for Banquo but Lady Macbeth has changed and now shows only a passing interest.

During the banquet scene we can almost feel sorry for her as she strives to stop Macbeth from revealing the truth. Once he has discovered that Fleance is still alive he becomes agitated but it is the knowledge of Banquo's death, although planned, that causes him to hallucinate and see the ghost. Lady Macbeth desperately tries to convince the thanes that his outpourings are due to a recurring illness and are nothing to worry about, while at the same time trying to calm Macbeth and jolt him back to sanity. She rebukes him sharply:

This is the very painting of your fear
This is the air drawn dagger which you said
Led you to Duncan.

However, as Macbeth's state of mind deteriorates yet further she realises that the situation is dangerous, for Macbeth has said too much already. When Ross asks, *What sights my lord?* Lady Macbeth acts swiftly: *Stand not upon the order of your going, but go at once.* She has striven to keep Macbeth from uttering damning comments and to restore him to normality, but has failed. When we consider that she also is feeling very depressed about what they have done, her efforts are heroic. She has the capacity to do what he cannot, to be unswerving and consistent, and not allow fanciful and fearful imagination control her words and actions in public. Yet, this same iron and rigid self control will finally break.

After their guests have gone she no longer chastises him, but simply sounds very weary, telling him that he *lacks the season of all natures, sleep.* Perhaps she is remembering Macbeth's words after the murder: *Macbeth shall sleep no more.*

Act 5

Lady Macbeth has come down a very long way from the determined, brisk, ruthless character of the early scenes in the play. Part of her distress must be put down to the fact that Macbeth, the focal point of her life, for whom she has plotted and schemed to raise to the highest position in the land, is now absent. She no longer knows his every move as she did before, and her life lacks meaning. Significantly, the gentlewoman says that Lady Macbeth has been sleepwalking since Macbeth *went into the field,* which indicates that he is away, fighting. He, however, is demonstrating the masculine qualities expected of Jacobean heroes and apparently no longer needs her, re asserting the male dominant approach to life as he single mindedly sets about suppressing all opposition.

In the sleepwalking scene Lady Macbeth's terror is revealed. All that she has suppressed during her support of her husband reveals itself in a tangle of fear and emotion. Yet, although her guilt is obvious, there is little sign of remorse. She re lives the night of the murder: *Who would have thought the old man to have so much blood in him?* and the memories of trying to rally her husband emerge: *Fie, a soldier and afeared?*

It is clear that she has heard rumours without being certain what has happened, as she ponders on what has happened to Lady Macduff: *Where is she now?* But it is the constant enacting of handwashing that gives the clearest indication of her troubled mind, and mocks her certainty of the murder night when she thought that the simple act would make everything easy, for now she laments: *What will these hands never be clean?*

Lady Macbeth is a complicated character. She has a deep, supportive love for her husband, and will stop at nothing to see that he achieves the greatest honour in the land. It is clear that she feels that she knows what is best for him and ruthlessly overcomes all his scruples and finer feelings. Her cruelty is immense, for her attitude towards Duncan is inhumane. But her inflexibilty breaks her finally, and she is unable to cope with her feelings of guilt and Macbeth's absence. Malcolm calls her *fiend-like,* a justified comment, and by committing suicide she commits the cardinal sin, while Macbeth fights to the end.

d. The Witches

The witches create confusion and uncertainty. In Jacobean England they were also feared to a great extent. Superstition was prevalent and lack of scientific knowledge fed erroneous ideas and fears. Those accused of being witches made useful scapegoats. James 1 fuelled these fears as he firmly believed that such beings existed with evil intent, and he wrote a book called *Daemonologie.* Its subject matter was the nature of hell, and he termed witches *the detestable slaves of the devil.* He was clear in his advice on how to run witch trials, encouraged the hounding of those termed witches, making the powerful argument to a religious nation that witchcraft was a sin against both king and God.

Primarily, women were seen as witches, which has connotations of the belief that women were temptresses and lured men to sin, dating back to Adam and Eve in the Garden of Eden.

Familiars, domestic pets, were meant to aid witches in their evil deeds, and many a hapless woman with a pet cat would be seen as a witch. Originally, witches were often seen as wise women, who would give advice on health and medicines, often being present to assist in childbirth. This developed into a suspicion of their expertise, and they were accused with little hope of justice.

What power does Shakespeare give the witches in this play? They appear to be able to predict the future, but that largely depends on how their prey reacts to their prophecies. They can only suggest; they cannot enforce. Macbeth acts on their suggestions, and Banquo fails to do the right thing, in the hope that if he doesn't share what he knows about Macbeth and the prophecies, and his belief that Macbeth acted upon those prophecies, then the predictions for his descendants would come true.

e. Banquo

Although Banquo is presented as an honourable character, his integrity slips when faced with temptation. The Banquo who warns Macbeth about the instruments of darkness begins to hope that their predictions will come true for him. A.C. Bradley considers that Banquo is the true victim of the witches.[53] Indeed, he never acts in such a way to harm others; his sin is one of omission in that he does not share his knowledge after the murder of Banquo, knowledge which might possibly have prevented much of the bloodshed that followed, and also have spared his life.

He is generous in his praise of Macbeth to Duncan even though all he receives from the king at that stage is thanks,

---

[53] A. C. Bradley 'Shakespearean Tragedy'

whereas Macbeth has been rewarded with the title of Thane of Cawdor, with promise of further honours.

He seems to have no fear of Macbeth, and this lack of guardedness gives Macbeth the time and opportunity to make plans to have him murdered. Banquo tells Macbeth that he dreamt of the witches, and as he has already revealed that he won't let himself sleep because of the thoughts that torture him, asking *merciful powers* to *restrain* in him *the cursed thoughts that nature gives way to in repose.*

Like Macbeth, Banquo gives way to ambition, although he is no villain. But the thought of his descendants becoming kings is too tempting to discount and he hopes that the witches will become his *oracles* and *set (him) up in hope*. His failure to act seals his fate.

f. Macduff

Usually, Shakespeare introduces his main characters and themes very early on in the play. However, Macduff proves an exception to the rule as we do not meet him until the end of Act 2. The reason is that Macduff is an avenger, entering the fray after Duncan's murder. He displays determination and courage, and almost from the moment of his discovery of Duncan's body, suspects Macbeth. His terse, *Wherefore did you then*?[54] when Macbeth expresses regret at killing the guards, also gives Macbeth and the audience early warning of Macduff's suspicions.

Macduff fails to come to court when commanded to do so, and then takes himself to England to persuade Malcolm to return and lead the fight against Macbeth. So eager is he to do so, that he leaves his wife and children unprotected, and Macbeth has them murdered.

Malcolm's wariness of Macduff's approaches fills Macduff with despair, and when Malcolm claims all manner

[54] Act 2 Scene 3

of iniquitous habits and behaviour, this drives Macduff to cry:

O nation miserable!
With an untitled tyrant bloody-sceptred,
When shalt thou see thy wholesome days again?

No sooner has Malcolm reassured him then Ross arrives with the terrible news of the slaughter of his family. Malcolm had asked earlier in the scene why *left you wife and child?* and now Macduff reproaches himself with:

Sinful Macduff,
[55]*They were all struck for thee!*

Macduff is not afraid to show emotion, despite the tough, masculine culture of the times, but his grief is soon joined by anger:

Front to front
Bring thou this fiend of Scotland and myself.

In the final battle Macduff reveals to Macbeth that he *was from his mother's womb untimely ripped*[56]destroying Macbeth's last hope of survival, despite the king's final defiant, *I will not yield to kiss the ground before young Malcolm's feet.*

With Macbeth's head held aloft, Macduff returns triumphantly to Malcolm, and proclaims him king, having gained his revenge and law, order and morality are restored once more.

---

[55] Act 4 Scene 3
[56] Act 5 Scene 7

g. Ross

Ross is ubiquitous in this play. He is present in many scenes often acting as a Greek chorus. He brings news to Duncan of the defeat of the King of Norway, and he bears the news to Macbeth that he is to be honoured with the title of Thane of Cawdor. He discusses the events after the murder of Duncan with an old man, being used by Shakespeare to give background information. We learn that he is to attend the coronation of Macbeth while Macduff will not.

In the banquet scene he is curious about the *sights* that Macbeth sees, and he visits Lady Macduff with the news that her husband has left Scotland. Whether it is Ross who tells her that Macduff has gone to England is not clear, but he is moved by her distress. He comments on the fact that *we are traitors* but do not know it, an allusion to the ruthlessness of Macbeth towards anyone he considers disloyal. His is the unenviable task of taking the news to Macduff in England that Macbeth has wiped out his family.

4. Themes and Imagery

The predominant imagery in this play is that of darkness: evil, malice, murder. Dowden considers that the message of the play can be summed up in the words *good things of day begin to droop and drowse.* [57] The deeds carried out by Macbeth and his wife, are so appalling, so evil, that it would seem that they can only be carried out under cover of darkness.

a. Darkness

a) In the scene where we first meet Macbeth, Banquo warns him about the *instruments of darkness.*[58] He is alluding to the witches and their deceitful promises.
b) After Duncan has named Malcolm as his heir, Macbeth, in an aside, pleads:
Let not light see my black and deep desires.[59]
c) Likewise, Lady Macbeth wishes for *thick night* and *the blanket of the dark*[60] to hide the murderous action she is planning.
d) It is dark when Banquo is talking to Fleance on the night of the murder. Fleance says *the moon is down* and Banquo comments that heaven's *candles are all out.*[61]
e) In his dagger soliloquy Macbeth muses on the fact that evil flourishes in darkness:
Nature seems dead, and wicked dreams abuse
The curtained sleep.

---

[57] Act 3 Scene 2 Also reference to 'Shakespeare's Imagery' Caroline Spurgeon

[58] Act 1 Scene 3

[59] Act 1 Scene 4

[60] Act 1 Scene 5

[61] Act 2 Scene 1

f) Lennox tells of the *unruly* night before Macduff discovers the body of Duncan. There were *strange screams of death* and the owl *clamoured the live-long night.*[62]

g) Ross discusses with the Old Man the fact that *dark night strangles the travelling lamp,* and *darkness does the face of earth entomb,*[63] suggesting that heaven and nature are deeply disturbed by Duncan's murder.

h) Banquo says he *must be a borrower of the night*[64] and this decision to ride back *in a dark hour* will seal his death warrant.

i) Macbeth tells the murderers that Banquo must be killed *tonight*[65] and Fleance also, *in a dark hour.*

j) Macbeth asks *seeling* (blinding) *night* to blindfold the eye of day, and as the *good things of day* begin to sleep, *night's black agents* become predatory.[66]

k) The first sign that the metaphorical night can be overcome is given to us by Malcolm. As he, Macduff, and an English army prepare to march to Scotland, he declares, *The night is long, that never finds the day.* [67]

b. Murder

a) The word *blood* is used throughout the play as an alternative to murder. The first time we hear Macbeth contemplating such an act is when he hears that the witches' prediction has partly come true, and that he is Thane of Cawdor. His own speculation creates a *horrid image* which makes his hair stand on end and

---

[62] Act 2 Scene 3
[63] Act 2 Scene 4
[64] Act 3 Scene 1
[65] Act 3 Scene 1
[66] Act 3 Scene 2
[67] Act 4 Scene 3

his heart thump. To become king he would have to murder the king, [68]although he has the faint hope that *chance may crown me without my stir* so that he can achieve his ambition without committing regicide. This is evocative of Lady Macbeth's conviction that although her husband would want to gain the kingship *holily* he would be happy to gain it unfairly: *wrongly win.*[69]

b) Lady Macbeth feels the need for the assistance from evil spirits to prevent *compunctious visitings of nature* shaking her *fell purpose* which is the murder of Duncan.[70]
c) In his soliloquy, where he considers murdering Duncan, Macbeth talks of *bloody* or murderous *instructions* which will *return to plague the inventor.*[71]
d) Lady Macbeth speaks of their anticipated *great quell* (murder) when explaining how the guards would be blamed.[72]
e) In the dagger soliloquy Macbeth comments that *the bloody business* is causing him to hallucinate and how night is appropriate for *withered murder.*[73]
f) Macbeth is full of remorse as soon as he has murdered Duncan and believes he hears a voice crying *Macbeth does murder sleep...Glamis hath murdered sleep.*[74]
g) Macduff's reaction when he finds Duncan's body is dramatic and one of absolute horror. He calls

---

[68] Act 1 Scene 3
[69] Act 1 Scene 5
[70] Act 1 Scene 5
[71] Act 1 Scene 7
[72] Act 1 Scene 7
[73] Act 2 Scene 1
[74] Act 2 Scene 2

Duncan's murder *sacrilegious*[75] for the king was seen as appointed by God.

h) Ironically, Macduff says he cannot repeat what has happened in front of Lady Macbeth as it would kill her ~ he uses the word *murder*. Twice in the next few lines Macduff again uses the word *murder*, firstly to Banquo and secondly, cutting through Macbeth's flowery words to say bluntly to Malcolm and Donalbain, *Your royal father's murdered.*[76]

i) Banquo calls Duncan's murder *this most bloody piece of work*, and he of all people must have very strong suspicions of Macbeth.

j) Donalbain realises how dangerous the position is for him and Malcolm, *the near in blood, the nearer bloody,* expressing the fear that as Duncan's sons they are in danger of being murdered next, while Malcolm responds metaphorically, commenting that *this murderous shaft* [77]has not yet landed.

k) In his soliloquy, expressing his fears over Banquo's nobility and what the witches have predicted, Macbeth muses over the fact that if that prediction comes true then he has murdered Duncan and given his soul to the devil for *Banquo's issue*. [78]The thought angers him and hardens his resolve to prevent the prophecy coming true.

l) Macbeth plans the murder of Banquo (and Fleance) and arranges with the murderers that it should happen that night, saying that he suffers while Banquo lives but his life *in his death were perfect.*[79]

---

[75] Act 2 Scene 3

[76] Act 2 Scene 3

[77]

[78] Act 3 Scene 1

[79] Act 3 Scene 1

m) Macbeth refers to the planned murder of Banquo as *a deed of dreadful note.*[80]
n) Macbeth sees the ghost of Banquo with *twenty mortal murders*[81] on his *crown* but this is probably hallucination because of fear and guilt. His imagination is plaguing him with *charnel houses,* and he reasons that if people are returning from their graves then *our monuments shall be the maws* (stomachs) *of kites.*
o) As Macbeth becomes more mired in his murderous, desperate acts, he realises that *blood will have blood,*[82] that murder will lead to more murder, and prophecies and related events will be revealed by crows and rooks, the foretellers of bad luck. He finishes the conversation with his wife by saying that he is *but young in deed,* chilling words that proclaim that far more murder will follow.
p) Macbeth plans to murder Lady Macduff and her children, a mindless, vindictive murder, and vows to *give to th' edge o' the sword*[83] all Macduff's descendants.
q) Macduff describes Macbeth as *an untitled tyrant, bloody-sceptred,*[84] alluding to the fact that Macbeth has no right to be on the throne and is using his power to murder to hold on to his position.
r) Later in the same scene Macduff receives the news that Macduff has had his wife and children murdered. Ross tells him, *Your wife and babes savagely slaughtered,* the alliteration emphasising the brutality.
s) Macbeth talks of his *slaughterous thoughts.*[85]

---

[80] Act 3 Scene 2
[81] Act 3 Scene 4
[82] Act 3 Scene 4
[83] Act 4 Scene 1
[84] Act 4 Scene 3
[85] Act 5 Scene 5

t) In their exchange before their final battle, Macbeth and Macduff both speak of murder, using the term *blood.* Macbeth is reluctant to fight Macduff as he feels that he has shed too much *blood* of Macduff's already, referring to the wholesale slaughter of Lady Macduff and her children. Macduff replies, calling Macbeth a *bloodier villain than terms can give thee out.* [86]

u) Malcolm labels Macbeth as a *butcher* in the final speech of the play, a fitting metaphor to summarise Macbeth's actions.

c. *The Supernatural*

The supernatural element in this play is largely symbolic of evil, especially where the witches are concerned. We do not know how far Shakespeare believed in witchcraft, and his psychological insights seem to outweigh such primitive beliefs. However, belief in witchcraft was the norm in Shakespearean England, James 1 was a fervent believer, and witchcraft was a capital offence. Several of Shakespeare's plays concern themselves with the supernatural, particularly ***Hamlet*** and ***Macbeth***.

a) We meet the witches in the first scene and learn that their natural environment is barren and stormy. We hear of their familiars and that anything *foul is fair* in their philosophy. Of greater interest and concern is their mention of Macbeth as this is a foreshadowing of something evil in his life, and that he is being targeted by the witches. As we do not know of Macbeth's overwhelming ambition at this stage in the play. we could also conjecture that they are eager to seduce an honourable man into acts of evil.

[86] Act 5 Scene 7

b) We meet the witches again in the third scene of the play, where the first witch boasts of her intention to punish the husband of a woman who refused to give her the chestnuts she was eating. The man, a captain of a trading ship was to suffer greatly, and would possibly die, as throughout a *weary sev'n-nights nine times nine* he would be so battered by winds from all directions that he would get no rest but would *dwindle, peak and pine*.

c) The meeting of Macbeth and Banquo with the witches, on the heath, is to prove momentous for both of them. The witches' predictions will lead to death and destruction, Macbeth slaughtering so many, including Banquo, who is a victim of his own ambition, failing to act on his belief that Macbeth murdered the king. Although Banquo warns Macbeth that *the instruments of darkness* seduce with minor truths to lure their victim, he allows the desire to see his descendants become kings to outweigh the fact that he should have acted to denounce Macbeth as guilty of regicide.

d) Lady Macbeth calls upon the supernatural, in the form of evil spirits, to fill her with evil, for she feels inadequate to fulfil her aims and hopes without such assistance. Her desire to be full of *direst cruelty*[87] is chilling, and she sounds sure that the *murd'ring ministers* are lurking invisibly to take advantage of when human beings have evil thoughts. She wishes that *thick night* should be shrouded in *the dunnest smoke of hell* so that heaven could not see the murder and prevent it.

e) In the dagger soliloquy[88] Macbeth muses on the fact that night is a time for evil acts and that the

---

[87] Act 1 Scene 5

[88] Act2 Scene 1

supernatural is in evidence as *witchcraft celebrates pale Hecate's offerings.*

f) Immediately after Duncan's murder, Macbeth is riddled with fear and remorse, and thinks he hears a voice crying that *Macbeth does murder sleep*. While lyrically extolling the virtues of sleep, he thinks that he will now be deprived of it for evermore, including all three titles to enforce the fact that he cannot be spared:
   Glamis hath murdered sleep, and therefore Cawdor
   Shall sleep no more. Macbeth shall sleep no more.[89]
g) Lennox speaks of the turbulent night of Duncan's murder and the reactions of nature and the supernatural. The night was *unruly',*[90] there were *strange screams of death* and the *obscure bird clamoured all night*, reminding us of the *fatal bellman*, the owl heard by Lady Macbeth.[91]
h) Ross, discussing the murder with an old man, comments that *the heavens* were *troubled with man's act.*[92]
i) Macbeth laments the fact that he has given his *eternal jewel* to the *common enemy of man,*[93] the devil, and wishes for fate to *champion* him to *th'utterance.*
j) The banquet scene [94] is momentous in that Macbeth is convinced that the ghost of Banquo is present, although he is the only person who can see him. Lady Macbeth, already under great strain herself, desperately tries to prevent him from revealing the truth to the nobles. Macbeth's complaint that Banquo has pushed him from his stool foreshadows the fact

---

[89] Act 2 Scene 2
[90] Act 2 Scene 3
[91] Act Scene 2
[92] Act 2 Scene 4
[93] Act 3 Scene 1
[94] Act 3 Scene 4

that Banquo's descendants would become kings, rather than his.

k) In the same scene Macbeth determines to seek out the witches.

l) Hecate, goddess of the moon and witchcraft, is angry with the witches for not only having dealings with Macbeth, but also for not including her so that she could *show the glory of our art.* [95] They will meet Macbeth at *the pit of Acheron,* which was probably the witches' cave, although the name originates from classical legend where it was one of the rivers of Hell.

m) The scene in which Macbeth meets the witches through his decision, is significant in that the apparitions will give him false hope and confidence, as he is told that he needs fear *none of woman born* and cannot be defeated until Birnam Wood comes to Dunsinane.[96] This gives him the security which Hecate terms *mortals' chiefest enemy.*[97] Macbeth is shown a procession of kings, symbolising Banquo's descendants, and calls the witches *filthy hags.* Despite the fact that the prediction about *none of woman born* can harm him has caused him to feel that he need have no fear of Macduff, Macbeth decides that he will make doubly sure and have him killed.

n) Macduff tells Malcolm that heaven was reacting to Scotland's woes *as if it felt with Scotland,*[98] uttering the same sorrowful cries.

o) Malcolm explains to Macduff the inexplicable power Edward the Confessor has in being able to cure diseased people *all swoll'n and ulcerous,*[99] and how he hangs a coin round their necks *put on with holy prayers.*

---

[95] Act 3 Scene 5
[96] Act 4 Scene 1
[97] Act 3 Scene 5
[98] Act 4 Scene 3
[99] Act 4 Scene 3

p) In the same scene Macduff asks why heaven looked on the murders of his wife and children and *would not take their part.*
q) In the sleepwalking scene the doctor talks of Lady Macbeth needing *the divine rather than the physician.*[100]

d. Clothes

There is much imagery surrounding clothing in this play.

a) When Ross tells Macbeth that he is to be honoured with the title of Thane of Cawdor, his response is one of bewilderment, asking, *Why do you address me in borrowed robes,*[101] as he has not heard of the treachery of the previous holder of the title.
b) Later in the same scene, Banquo surmises that Macbeth's spellbound state is due to his *new honours,* that like new clothes, will only fit comfortably when he is used to them.
c) Macbeth tells his wife that he will not be murdering Duncan because his honours *should be worn now in their newest gloss.*[102]
d) Lady Macbeth's response is caustic: *Was the hope drunk, wherein you dressed yourself?*
e) Macduff comments ironically on Macbeth's coronation, *Lest our old robes sit easier than our new,*[103] as his suspicions are already heightened.
f) Angus reflects upon Macbeth's state of mind as the united Scottish/English army draws near, and concludes that the title of king,
Hangs loose upon him, like a giant's robe
Upon a dwarfish thief.[104]

[100] Act 5 Scene 1
[101] Act 1 Scene 3
[102] Act 1 Scene 7
[103] Act 2 Scene 4
[104] Act 5 Scene 2

The implication is that not only has Macbeth gained the throne corruptly, but that also he lacks the kingly qualities to rule, perhaps an implicit reference to the way that Duncan had been regarded.

e. Ambition

The O.E.D. defines ambition as *a strong desire to do or achieve something, or a desire and determination to achieve success.*

Ambition is the major theme in this play as it is the cause of Macbeth's downfall. But it is a many factored word and Macdonwald the rebel, the original Thane of Cawdor who assists the King of Norway, the Norwegian king himself, the malicious witches, all these have ambition. Lady Macbeth also has ambition, but it is for her husband, not herself. We will look at the more overt statements of ambition.

a) Macbeth's ambition is hinted at when he hears the witches' predictions.[105] Banquo expresses surprise at the fact that Macbeth is startled, and the reason for Macbeth's reaction becomes clearer when, after Ross tells him that he is Thane of Cawdor, he begins to speculate about becoming king, albeit fearfully. He also considers that *the greatest is behind*, which is surprising when he is Thane of Glamis through birth, and Thane of Cawdor as a gift from the king. To [106]jump from there to the position of king is a tremendous leap.
b) Macbeth receives the news that Malcolm will be Duncan's heir as a challenge, and asks, *Let not light see my black and deep desires*.[107] Irony is always

---

[105] Act 1 Scene 3
[106] Act 1 Scene 3
[107] Act 1 Scene 4

present in this play, and while he is thinking that, Duncan and Banquo are praising him.

c) Lady Macbeth concedes that Macbeth has *ambition, but without the illness should attend it,* [108]meaning he lacks the wickedness necessary. She is determined that he *shalt be what thou art promised.* Her ambition for him is taken to new heights when she invokes evil spirits to help her achieve her murderous aims.

d) In his first soliloquy Macbeth gives careful thought to murdering Duncan and comes to the conclusion that he had no *spur* to drive him to act except for:
Vaulting ambition, which o'erleaps itself,
And falls on the other. [109]
Therefore, he knows, even before the murder that he is aiming too high.

e) Lady Macbeth is not happy when her husband tells her that he does not want to go ahead with the murder, calls him a coward and mocks the ambition he had shown before, asking if he had been drunk when he suggested the assassination. *Nor time not place did then adhere*[110]but he had been determined to make both, only to back out now the opportunity had arisen.

f) Banquo, too, has ambition, for his descendants to become kings as the witches had predicted. This ambition is to prove his downfall, and reveals him in a less than honourable light as it prevents him from denouncing Macbeth as a murderer. Instead, he hopes the witches will be his *oracles as well,*[111] and give him hope.

---

[108] Act 1 Scene 5
[109] Act 1 Scene 7
[110] Act 1 Scene 7
[111] Act 3 Scene 1

f. Sleep

a) The first mention of sleep is when the first witch vows that the sailor husband of the woman, who refused to give her chestnuts, will be denied sleep for *sev'n-nights nine times nine.*[112]
b) Lady Macbeth talks of the planned murder of Duncan, terming it *this night's great business.*[113]
c) The murder of Duncan is planned for when he is asleep.[114]
d) Banquo finds thoughts of the witches, probably their predictions, deeply disturbing, so much so that he is afraid to sleep, because of *the cursed thoughts that nature gives way to in repose.*[115] He tells Macbeth that he dreamed of the witches the previous night.
e) Macbeth soliloquises about the fact that the night is conducive to evil acts, when half the world was dead and *wicked dreams abuse the curtained sleep.*[116]
f) Lady Macbeth has drugged Duncan's guards and they are *quenched* to such an extent that:
   Death and nature do contend about them
   Whether they live or die.[117]
g) After the murder Macbeth hears one of Duncan's sons laugh in his sleep, and the other cried, *Murder!* He then says he hears a voice cry:
   Sleep no more,
   Macbeth does murder sleep.[118]
   He speaks lyrically and metaphorically of sleep and its benefits and virtues, and finishes in despair:
   Glamis hath murdered sleep, and therefore Cawdor

---

[112] Act 1 Scene 3
[113] Act 1 Scene 5
[114] Act 1 Scene 6
[115] Act 2 Scene 1
[116] Act 2 Scene 1
[117] Act 2 Scene 2
[118] Act 2 Scene 2

Shall sleep no more. Macbeth shall sleep no more.

h) Lady Macbeth, who has no understanding of how her husband feels, then tells him impatiently that *the sleeping and the dead are but as pictures*.

i) Macbeth talks of the *terrible dreams that shake* (him) *nightly*, almost envying Duncan for the fact that *he sleeps well* for *nothing can touch him further.*[119]

j) After the banquet scene, when Macbeth is planning to visit the witches, Lady Macbeth, herself under tremendous strain, tells him that he *lacks the season of all nature's sleep.*[120]

k) A lord, talking to Lennox, longs for the time when they would be able to give *'sleep to our nights.*[121]

l) Macbeth believes that with the threat of Macduff gone he will be able to *sleep in spite of thunder.*[122]

m) Lady Macbeth literally sleepwalks her way through Act 5 Scene 1, as she re lives the terrible night of Duncan's murder.

g. Sexual Stereotyping

Shakespeare frequently has women play roles outside those expected of them in Elizabethan and Jacobean England. In plays such as ***The Merchant of Venice, Much Ado about Nothing,*** and ***Antony and Cleopatra,*** the woman plays a dominant role. In ***Macbeth*** Lady Macbeth sees femininity as weakness, a reflection of the society in which she lives. She attempts to reject her feminine qualities, while urging her husband to accept the masculine stereotype of aggression and violence when he wavers in his intention to murder Duncan, taunting him with cowardice. From the beginning of the play we hear, through the words of others,

119 Act 3 Scene 2

120 Act 3 Scene 4

121 Act 3 Scene 6

122 Act 4 Scene 1

of the ruthlessness, boldness and brutality of Macbeth, perceived as excellent, desirable qualities.

a) Macbeth is seen as an archetypal captain, fearless, courageous, resolute. Fighting Macdonwald, not only is his sword *smoked with bloody execution* but he is personified as *Valour's minion.*[123] The double meaning of *execution* emphasises the power and ruthlessness of the man, as does his act of slicing Macdonwald open from *the nave to the chaps*.

b) The rest of the scene is also concerned with impressing upon us how brave Macbeth is, the epitome of what a man at the time should be. The Norwegian king, Sweno, aided by the Thane of Cawdor, attacked *with furbished arms.*[124]However, Macbeth and Banquo prove more than capable of dealing with the situation, especially Macbeth, *Bellona's bridegroom*.

c) Ross tells Macbeth how grateful Duncan is for Macbeth's success in the *kingdom's great defence*, and how the messengers had all told of Macbeth being *nothing afeared of what thyself didst make.* [125] The picture has been built up of a ruthless, reckless man, loyal to king and country.

d) The Thane of Cawdor dies bravely and honourably, imploring Duncan's pardon with *deep repentance*. [126]Again, this is typical of how a noble man should die.

e) Lady Macbeth wishes to throw off her feminine traits and is desperate for evil spirits to fill her from head to toe with *direst cruelty.* [127] A symbol of a nurturing woman, her milk, she wishes to change for bitter gall.

---

[123] Act 1 Scene 2
[124] Act 1 Scene 2
[125] Act 1 Scene 3
[126] Act 1 Scene 4
[127] Act 1 Scene 5

f) When Macbeth decides to proceed no further with the murder of Duncan, Lady Macbeth is full of contempt and mocks him for being a coward. He is stung, and responds immediately, *I dare do all that may become a man.*[128] She taunts him by saying that he was a man when he first proposed the idea of murdering Duncan, but the fact that it is now possible to do so has *unmade* him. Had she broken such a vow she would have committed the ultimate horrific act of dashing the brains out of her baby as it fed from her breast, a stark rejection of her femininity, tenderness and humanity, demonstrating the masculine qualities she is accusing him of lacking. Her passion, derision and argument convince Macbeth to go ahead with the murder.

g) Lady Macbeth reveals glimmers of humanity when she is unable to kill Duncan as *he resembled (her) father as he slept*[129] but is quick to condemn her husband's remorse after the murder. She describes him as being *brainsickly* and having *a heart so white*, as his *constancy has left (him) unattended.*

h) There is irony in Macduff feeling unable to speak of the murder in front of a woman, and Lady Macbeth's fainting, whether genuine or contrived, is indicative of perceived feminine frailty. However, in Macbeth's killing of Duncan's guards, we see the resurgence of his ruthless nature.

i) Macbeth tells Banquo's ghost that he would willingly fight him to the death if he were alive. *What man dare, I dare* [130] has connotations of his quick response to Lady Macbeth's taunts of cowardice.

---

[128] Act 1 Scene 7
[129] Act 2 Scene 2
[130] Act 3 Scene 4

j) Macduff comments on the fact that he and Malcolm *like good men* should *bestride our downfall'n birthdom.*[131]
k) Malcolm urges Macduff in his grief *to dispute it like a man.*[132]
l) The soldier in Macbeth asserts itself as he vows, *I'll fight till from my bones my flesh be hacked.*[133]
m) Again, Macbeth cries, *Blow, wind! Come, wrack! At least we'll die with harness on our back.*[134]
n) Siward is content when he learns that his son has died bravely. He refers to Young Siward as *God's soldier* and that he could not wish any son *a fairer death.*[135]

h. Deceit

Deceit runs throughout the play, a predominant theme, like murder.

a) The witches deceive Macbeth with equivocation.
b) Macbeth is warned of the witches' deceit by Banquo for they tell trivial truths in order to gain our trust then *betray's in deepest consequence.*[136]
c) Duncan comments on the deceit of the Thane of Cawdor whom he had *built an absolute trust,* saying *there's no art to find the mind's construction in the face.*[137]
d) Macbeth replies to Duncan's praise of his battle achievements with courteous standard phrasing, while harbouring treasonous thoughts. When he learns that Malcolm is to be named Prince of

---

131 Act 4 Scene 3
132 Act 4 Scene 3
133 Act 5 Scene 3
134 Act 5 Scene 5
135 Act 5 Scene 8
136 Act 1 Scene 3
137 Act 1 Scene 4

Cumberland, the king's heir, he is frightened of his own thoughts: *Yet let that be*
Which the eye fears when it is done to see.[138]

e) Lady Macbeth advises her husband that if he is to deceive he must behave normally, saying, *To beguile the time,*
Look like the time.[139]
To her Macbeth is transparent, she can read him like a book. He must really act honestly and openly*: Look like th'innocent flower,*
But be the serpent under it.
f) When Duncan arrives at her castle in Inverness, Lady Macbeth flatters him, telling him that even if her service towards him was done twice and then doubled it would be inadequate in comparison to the honours Duncan has conferred in the past.[140]
g) After Lady Macbeth has persuaded Macbeth finally to go along with her plan, Macbeth says that he is ready to proceed with the *terrible feat* and knows that he must deceive others as to his intentions: *False face must hide what the false heart doth know.*[141]
h) Macbeth tells a troubled Banquo that he does not think about the witches, after Banquo has told him that he dreamed of the witches the night before.[142]
i) Macbeth makes a contrived, hyperbolic speech about the reasons he killed Duncan's guards. [143]
j) Macbeth tries to deceive the nobles by maintaining that Malcolm and Donalbain bribed the guards to murder Duncan. He says that the brothers are not confessing their crime but are

---

[138] Act 1 Scene 4
[139] Act 1 Scene 5
[140] Act 1 Scene 6
[141] Act 1 Scene 7
[142] Act 1 Scene 7
[143] Act 2 Scene 3

filling their hearers
With strange invention.[144]

k) Macbeth persuades the murderers that Banquo has been responsible for their past misfortunes.[145]
l) Macbeth reminds his wife that they must continue to deceive people; they must *make our faces vizards (masks) to our hearts.*[146]
m) The witches deceive Macbeth. (See equivocation theme)
n) Malcolm deceives Macduff by claiming several vices for himself, to test whether Macduff is genuine. Once he realises that Macduff is on his side he reveals why he has done that: Macbeth has 'sought to win me into his power' by sending men to tempt him back to Scotland with promises of support.

i. Time

a) The first allusion to time is made by the witches when they determine to meet *ere the set of sun.*[147] Ominously, it is to meet Macbeth.
b) Again, time is mentioned by the witches, when they tell Macbeth he *shalt be king hereafter.*[148]
c) In the same scene, Banquo wonders whether the witches *can look into the seeds of time.*
d) As he contemplates the possible murder of Duncan, Macbeth declares in an aside, *Time and the hour runs through the roughest day.*[149] Later in the play, Malcolm comments, as he and Macduff prepare to leave England for Scotland, to avenge the murder and

---

144 Act 3 Scene 1
145 Act 3 Scene 1
146 Act 3 Scene 2
147 Act 1 Scene 1
148 Act 1 Scene 3
149 Act 1 Scene 3

claim the throne as rightfully his, *The night is long, that never finds the day.*[150]

e) Duncan's timing of his visit to Inverness, Macbeth's castle, is very ill-timed, ironically decided because of Macbeth's service to him.[151]
f) A decisive Lady Macbeth feels 'the future in the instant' and talks of coming events as '*this night's great business*' *and anticipates their future:*
All our nights and days to come
Give solely sovereign sway and masterdom.
g) Contemplating whether to murder Duncan, Macbeth thinks about *this bank and shoal of time*, life on earth as contrasted with eternity, *the life to come.*[152] If he could have success in the present he would ignore the future.
h) Lady Macbeth considers that the time and place is perfect for the murder, looking back to the time when Macbeth was determined to *make both* despite the fact that neither were feasible.[153]
i) Macbeth avers that if he *had died an hour before this chance,* he had *lived a blessed time.*[154] This is probably the last genuine public speech he will make, and his remorse is palpable immediately after the murder.
j) Macbeth is shown the future with Banquo's descendants occupying both the thrones of Scotland and England: *Some I see*
that twofold balls and treble sceptres carry.[155]
k) Macbeth laments, *Time, thou anticipat'st my dread exploits* [156]when he learns that Macduff has 'fled' to

---

[150] Act 5 Scene 1
[151] Act 1 Scene 5
[152] Act 1 Scene 7
[153] Act 1 Scene 7
[154] Act 2 Scene 3
[155] Act 4 Scene 1
[156] Act 4 Scene 1

England. He had planned to have Macduff killed to make sure that he could not be a threat to him, despite being assured by the witches that *none of woman born* could harm him.

l) Macbeth ponders on time and the brevity and futility of life. We are actors, someone who *struts and frets his hour upon the stage,*
And then is heard no more.[157]

m) Malcolm brings order back once more to Scotland, and states his aim to carry out necessary duties *in measure, time and place.*[158]

j. Equivocation

Equivocation, broadly speaking, is the use of ambiguous language to conceal the truth or to avoid committing oneself. In this play equivocation is widely used by characters including the witches, Lady Macbeth, Ross, Malcolm and Macbeth himself. A reference to a topical event is made by the Porter in his grimly, dark comedy scene.

a) The prediction that Macbeth shall be Thane of Cawdor is an illustration of Banquo's assertion that *the instruments of darkness...win us with honest trifle*[159]to then deceive us over deadly matters. *King hereafter* is such. The witches play lethal games with their equivocation.

b) Sleep too has its ambiguities. Although Macbeth is lyrical about its qualities [160]he also recognises its double nature in that it brings him terrible nightmares, commenting that it would be better to be dead than suffer as he now does, for Duncan *sleeps well* now he is dead.

---

[157] Act 5 Scene 5
[158] Act 5 Scene 8
[159] Act 1 Scene 3
[160] Act 2 Scene 2

c) In his first main soliloquy Macbeth ponders on the double nature of justice in that it *returns to plague th'inventor.*[161]
d) The Porter talks of an equivocator who could not *equivocate himself to heaven.*[162] This is thought to be a reference to the Jesuit, Father Henry Garnet, who thought he furthered God's ends by giving ambiguous answers when arrested on suspicion of following an illegal religion. This way he could avoid self recrimination, but eventually he was condemned to death. He was put to death in 1606
e) In his first main soliloquy Macbeth ponders on the double nature of justice in that it *returns to plague th'inventor.*[163]
f) When Macbeth visits the witches at the Pit of Acheron he is assured that no man born of woman could harm him, and that he could not be defeated until Great Birnam Wood would come to Dunsinane. Later he learns that the wood appears to be approaching Dunsinane. His conviction loses its certainty and he begins *to doubt th' equivocation of the fiend that lies like truth.*[164]
g) When Macduff reveals to Macbeth that he was *from his mother's womb untimely ripped,*[165] Macbeth initially feels that all the fight has drained from him. He curses Macduff for telling him and says of the witches:
Be these juggling fiends no more believed
That palter with us in a double sense.[166]

---

[161] Act 1 Scene 7
[162] Act 2 Scene 3
[163] Act 1 Scene 7
[164]

[165] Act 5 Scene 7
[166] Act 5 Scene 3

h) Ross is reluctant to break the news of the slaughter of Macduff's family. He prevaricates for a while, saying *they were well at peace when I did leave them.*[167]

[167] Act 4 Scene 3

5. Language

'Macbeth', like all of Shakespeare's plays is rich in figurative language. His use of metaphor, including personification, is evident throughout. Frequently we encounter a stream of lyrical, powerful language:

Methought I heard a voice cry, 'Sleep no more:
Macbeth does murder sleep', the innocent sleep,
Sleep that knits up the ravell'd sleeve of care,
The death of each day's life, sore labour's bath,
Balm of hurt minds, great nature's second course,
Chief nourisher in life's feast.[168]

The play is mostly written in blank verse: iambic pentameter that does not rhyme. Iambic pentameter consists of a line of ten syllables and is thought to be the closest in form to natural speech, with an iam, or foot, comprised of two syllables, with the stress falling on the second syllable. Blank verse is used for all the soliloquies and significant speeches, giving a sense of grandeur to the words.

Shakespeare ends some significant scenes with a rhyming couplet, which gives a dramatic, satisfying conclusion. It can pose a warning or prediction:

Hear it not Duncan, for it is a knell
That summons thee to heaven or to hell.[169]

Again, when contemplating the murder of Banquo:

...Banquo, thy soul's flight
If it find heaven, must find it out tonight.[170]

---

[168] Act 2 Scene 2
[169] Act 3 Scene 1
[170] Act 3 Scene 2

The witches mostly speak in rhyme and this fits in well with their chanting of spells and incantations, and also their paradoxical language:

Fair is foul and foul is fair,
Hover through the fog and filthy air.

The fact that Macbeth uses rhyme more than any other character, highlights an affinity with the witches.

Shakespeare uses prose for lesser characters, characters without social standing, or in a situation which deviates from normal behaviour. There are only four occasions in the play where prose is used:

1. Lady Macbeth (Act 1 Scene 5) ~ the letter has a sense of grim foreshadowing.
2. The Porter (Act 2 Scene 3) ~ the Porter's drunken words are a prelude to Macduff finding the murdered king.
3. The conversation between Lady Macduff and her son (Act 4 Scene 2) ~ mother and son sparring builds up the tension to their inevitable murder.
4. The sleepwalking scene (Act 5 Scene 1) this is chilling in its revelations and presentation of a diseased, distraught mind.

At times the language becomes broken and urgent, a reflection of the state of mind of the speaker. The stichomythia (dramatic dialogue in which two characters answer each other rapidly in alternating single lines) employed by Macbeth and his wife immediately after the murder of Duncan is an excellent example:

L.M. *Did not you speak?*
M. *When?*
L.M. *Now.*
M. *As I descended?*
L.M. *Ay.*

The jagged, abrupt tone reflects their fear and agitation. Lady Macbeth is quick to recover her composure, composure that her tormented husband cannot achieve, but at this moment she, too, is caught up in the enormity of their deed.

6. Shakespeare's source for Macbeth ~ History and Holinshed

a. History

History tells us that Duncan was a weak, ineffectual king, and that Macbeth probably had an equal claim to the throne. He was descended from Malcolm 2nd, and was married to Gruach who was the granddaughter of a High King of Scotland. Under the rules of tanistry, accession to the throne could include being descended from both male or female members of the Royal family, although only a male could become king.

Macbeth was born in 1005, (approximately) the son of the King of Moray. His father was the grandson of Malcolm 1, and his mother was the daughter of the ruling king, Malcom 2nd. He was married to Gruach, the granddaughter of a High King of Scotland. Thus, Macbeth had a strong claim to the throne.

In 1034 Malcolm 2nd died, and Duncan, his grandson came to the throne. Macbeth apparently did not contest this. Duncan was about four years older than Macbeth, not the elderly idealised monarch portrayed by Shakespeare. He was an ineffective warrior, and when he invaded the Kingdom of Moray in 1040, Macbeth's territory, he was killed in battle. It is not known if it was Macbeth who killed him.

Macbeth then became king, and was strong and successful. After ruling for seventeen years, Macbeth was faced with attack from Duncan's son, Malcolm. He had only been nine-years-old when his father had been killed. Now, with the help of Edward the Confessor, he invaded the Scotland of Macbeth, and the ageing king, now over fifty-years-old, was killed at the Battle of Lumphanan.

Macbeth's allies put his inadequate stepson, Lulach, on the throne, but he was a failure, easily defeated and killed a year later, in another battle with Malcolm.

Regicide was very common, but Malcolm managed to hold on to his throne, but was now under the influence and virtual control of an English king. This interference of the English in Scottish affairs lasted until James V1 became James 1 of England and united the two kingdoms. By this time, primogeniture, the accession of the eldest son, was the norm.

b. Holinshed's Version

In 1577, Raphael Holinshed wrote ***The Chronicles of Scotland***. Although these chronicles are not considered to be historically accurate, they are interesting and entertaining, and were the primary source for Shakespeare's ***Macbeth,*** Shakespeare following Holinshed's account very closely. The Chronicles give an outline of Macbeth's first meeting with the witches up until Macduff killed him. Duncan was not the only king to be murdered by someone he trusted, for Holinshed records also the murder of King Duff in the home of a subject whom he trusted and respected.

Holinshed tells us that as Macbeth and Banquo made their way to Forres, they met *three women in strange and wild apparel* who prophesied that Macbeth would become Thane of Glamis, Thane of Cawdor and King. Banquo then asked about his fortune and was told that he would benefit more than Macbeth, for the latter would come to an *unlucky end* without children to succeed him. Banquo would not reign but his descendants would *govern the Scottish kingdom by long order of continual descent.*

Soon after this, the existing Thane of Cawdor was executed for treason and Macbeth was awarded with all that Cawdor had possessed. And although Shakespeare's Banquo remained a serious character, Holinshed portrayed him as jesting with Macbeth that he now only had to obtain the kingship.

Macbeth began to think seriously about the matter and was *sore troubled* by Malcolm being proclaimed as Duncan's heir. Macbeth achieved this with the assistance of his ambitious wife who had '*an unquenchable desire to bear the name of queen'*. However, Shakespeare portrays her as being ambitious for her husband alone.

Macbeth murdered the king and was then proclaimed king in Duncan's place, causing Malcolm and Donalbain to flee for fear of their lives. Malcolm was given *most friendly entertainment* by King Edward, and Donalbain was *tenderly cherished* by the King of Ireland.

in Shakespeare's play Macbeth probably ruled for a few months only, Holinshed related that he *governed the realm for a space of ten years in equal justice before he began to show what he was.* He became afraid that he would suffer the same fate as his predecessor. He was also plagued by the witches' prediction for Banquo and arranged for him, and his son Fleance, to be murdered on their way to supper with him. Fleance escaped.

After this, everything began to go wrong for Macbeth and he became a man to be feared. Although he was warned by *certain wizards* to be wary of Macduff, a witch told him that he would not be killed by any man born of woman, or until Birnam Wood came to Dunsinane Castle. This reassured him.

Macduff went to England to persuade Malcolm to claim the Scottish crown. As Macbeth had spies in all the noblemen's houses he learned of this, and for spite had Macduff's wife, children, and all other occupants of his castle, killed. He labelled Macduff as a traitor and confiscated his land and goods.

Meanwhile, Macduff, unaware of all this, was acquainting Malcolm with the woes of Scotland. But Malcolm was wary, wondering if Macbeth had sent Macduff to England to lure him back. Malcolm pretended to be lustful, avaricious, and lacking in all the virtues necessary for a noble, virtuous king. Here, Holinshed was followed very closely by Shakespeare.

Macduff poignantly expressed his grief that Scotland would be exchanging a tyrant for another unsuited to the throne; Malcolm realised that he was genuine and retracted all he had said in condemnation of himself.

Macduff returned to Scotland to rally the forces there, while Malcolm arranged with King Edward for Siward, Earl of Northumberland, and an army of ten thousand men, to accompany him to Scotland and join with the Scottish rebels against Macbeth.

Macbeth was still convinced that the prophecies were accurate, and that he, therefore, was safe. Malcolm, arriving in Scotland soon after Macduff, ordered his army to cut down branches from the trees in Birnam Wood to conceal the true number of soldiers.

Macbeth *marvelled what the matter meant* when he saw the *trees* approaching, but then remembered the prophecy. However, he ordered his men to fight bravely.

Macduff *pursued* Macbeth who called him a *traitor* and said that he couldn't be *slain by any creature that is born of woman*. Macduff then informed him that he *was never born of (his) mother, but ripped out of her womb*. Macduff then approached Macbeth, *slew him in the place,* and cut off his head and mounted it on a pole.

Malcolm was duly crowned at Scone and rewarded all those who had helped him. He also created the first earls known in Scotland.

When Siward learned that his dead son had received his wounds to the front of his body in the battle, he said, *I rejoice even with all my heart, for I would not wish neither to my son nor to myself any other kind of death.*

Rarely does Shakespeare deviate from Holinshed's account, but he makes the characters vivid and fascinating, presenting them as both credible and convincing. He was happy to take someone else's version of a tale, real or imagined, and then transform it into a masterpiece.

7. Plan for Macbeth essay:

Starting with this moment in the play, explore how Shakespeare presents the attitudes of Macbeth and Banquo towards the supernatural: Act 1 Scene 3 lines 40-130.

Firstly, you need to examine the extract given very carefully, and analyse the immediate reactions and attitudes of the characters. It is a good idea to reveal your wider knowledge of the play by cross referencing to support a point as I have done in paragraph 1.

Don't tell the story.

Then move on to what we learn of their attitudes towards the supernatural in the rest of the play, comparing these attitudes.

Don't include anything irrelevant. It would be tempting to write about Lady Macbeth's attitude here, but there would be no marks for it.

Plan

Initially we learn that Banquo is cynical about the supernatural, considering that *the instruments of darkness* seduce people into trusting them by tempting them with trivial truths. Darkness is a theme that occurs frequently in this play and Macbeth asks that *light not see my black and deep desires* and muses upon the supernatural in the form of Hecate and witchcraft being active at night.

It is clear that Macbeth pays no heed to Banquo's warning as he ponders upon the supernatural, juxtaposing the *ill* and the *good*, and finding no answers to his dilemma. But it is the good aspect that troubles him most as it does not fit comfortably with his imagination. He finds that *yield(ing)* to the *suggestion* distresses him greatly, and the fact that the *horrid image* makes his hair stand on end and his heart thump is evidence of his faith in the supernatural, as the possibility of murdering Duncan shatters his equilibrium. There is despair in the words *nothing is, but what is not* and the paradox is evidence of his confusion as he wrestles with his conscience.

Elsewhere in the play:

Although Banquo advises Macbeth to be wary of the witches we find that he has also been seduced by their prophecies. Thoughts of what the witches have said cause him to plead with God to take away the *cursed thoughts that nature gives way to in repose*. Therefore, he finds himself unable to rest as he is plagued by the thoughts of his descendants becoming kings, knowing that for that to happen Duncan would have to be murdered.

After Duncan's murder he has little to say, but we discover his thoughts in his soliloquy and his hopes that as the witches' prophecies for Macbeth have come true, they might also come true for him: *Myself should be the root and father of many kings.* Therefore, despite his earlier warning to Macbeth, the witches have affected him deeply and this has overruled his scruples as he hopes to benefit from the king's murder.

Macbeth accepts the witches' prophecies from the moment he is given them, and this belief is possibly fuelled by earlier considerations of killing Duncan for his fearful reaction to the witches' words is observed by Banquo. In the banquet scene Macbeth believes he sees Banquo's ghost and becomes desperate to seek reassurance from the supernatural, accepting without question the promises that *none of woman born* can harm him, and that until Birnam Wood moves to Dunsinane he is safe. By this time he has sold his soul to the devil and knows it, throwing his lot in with the supernatural and holding on to their words with increasing desperation until he finally realises that they 'palter' with words and have deceived him.

This is just a sample of points that could be included in the essay. Resist the temptation just to re tell the story, and COMMENT on what happens instead. The word HOW in the question means comment on the language, motives, hopes and fears of the characters.

8. Literary Terms and Useful Words and Phrases for Essays

a. *Literary Terms*

Alliteration

Sometimes termed 'initial rhyme'. This is the same consonant sound at the beginning of two or more words that are close together. Some are plosive, such as *It is the **bloody business** which informs thus to my eyes.*

Metaphor

A form of imagery which compares and describes by saying it is something else. It is the most powerful form of figurative language. Shakespeare's plays are rich in metaphor.

*It was the owl that shrieked, **the fatal bellman**.*
We have scorched the snake, not killed it.

Personification

A figure of speech in which animals, abstract ideas and anything inanimate are referred to in human terms.

Was the hope drunk,
Wherein you dressed yourself? Hath it slept since?
I think our country sinks beneath the yoke,
It weeps, it bleeds…

Simile

Another form of imagery, not as powerful as the metaphor, but nevertheless highly effective in Shakespeare's hands, in which direct comparison is made.

Then comes my fit again. I had else been perfect;
Whole as the marble, founded as the rock;
As broad and general as the casing air.
Macbeth then moves on to express himself in metaphor:
But now I am cabined, cribbed, confined, bound in
To saucy doubts and fears.

Paradox
A contradictory statement which makes sense when a deeper meaning is sought. Shakespeare uses **chiasmus,** a form of paradox in which clauses are reversed, to highlight the ambiguity of the witches:

> ***Fair is foul and foul is fair.***

Macbeth echoes these words just before he meets the witches for the first time:

> ***So fair and foul a day I have not seen.***

Oxymoron
A compressed form of paradox.

> ***Joyful trouble.***

Stichomythia
Dialogue in which two characters respond to each other rapidly in alternating single lines. (See language section, page 73)

b. Useful words and phrases for essays

suggests
demonstrates
evokes
presents
implies
we infer from this that…
illustrates
highlights
focuses on
discusses
connotes
emphasises
evidence of
clarifies
causes us to consider

reinforces the idea that…
reiterates the fact that…
alludes to the fact that…
explains
explores

www.ingramcontent.com/pod-product-compliance
Ingram Content Group UK Ltd.
Pitfield, Milton Keynes, MK11 3LW, UK
UKHW040010200726
13854UKWH00001B/131

9 781803 692661